D0483779

A Brief History of Vatican II

A Brief History of Vatican II

Giuseppe Alberigo

Translated by
Matthew Sherry

ORBIS BOOKS

Maryknoll, New York 10545

Founded in 1970, Orbis Books endeavors to publish works that enlighten the mind, nourish the spirit, and challenge the conscience. The publishing arm of the Maryknoll Fathers and Brothers, Orbis seeks to explore the global dimensions of the Christian faith and mission, to invite dialogue with diverse cultures and religious traditions, and to serve the cause of reconciliation and peace. The books published reflect the opinions of their authors and are not meant to represent the official position of the Maryknoll Society. To obtain more information about Maryknoll and Orbis Books, please visit our website at www.maryknoll.org.

English translation copyright © 2006 by Orbis Books, Maryknoll, New York, U.S.A.

This book is a translation of the original Italian edition of the book, *Breve Storia del Concilio Vaticano II (1959-1962)*, copyright © 2005 by Società editrice Mulino, Bologna (Italy) by Matthew Sherry. For more on the Mulino publishing program see www.mulino.it.

No part of this publication may be reproduced or transmitted in any form or by any means, electronic or mechanical, including photocopying, recording, or any information storage or retrieval system, without prior permission in writing from the publishers. For permissions, write to Orbis Books, P.O. Box 308, Maryknoll NY 10545-0308, U.S.A.

Cover: On 25 December 1961 Pope John XXIII signs the document convoking Vatican Council II (photo from Catholic News Service).

Manufactured in the United States of America.
English manuscript editing and typesetting by Joan Weber Laflamme.

Library of Congress Cataloging-in-Publication Data

Alberigo, Giuseppe.
    [Breve storia del Concilio Vaticano II. English]
    A brief history of Vatican II / Giuseppe Alberigo ; translated by Matthew Sherry.
    p. cm.
    Includes bibliographical references and index.
    ISBN-13: 978–1–57075–638–2 (pbk.)
  1. Vatican Council (2nd : 1962–1965) I. Title.
  BX8301962 .A55 2006
  262'.52—dc22

                                                2005035076

Contents

Foreword

John W. O'Malley, SJ

No historian is better qualified to comment on Vatican II than Giuseppe Alberigo. He is most widely known as the editor of the five-volume history of the Council translated into the major European languages and published in English by Orbis Books under the able editorship of Joseph A. Komonchak of The Catholic University of America. Alberigo gathered the international team of scholars who contributed to the volumes and with his collaborators in Bologna saw this complex and daunting project to completion. That history will remain for generations the first source to which scholars will turn to initiate them into the dynamics of the Council and into the ambiguities and tensions of its course from the moment it was announced on January 25, 1959, until it completed its business on December 8, 1965. For Alberigo those volumes are the fitting culmination of a lifetime of reflection and research on what has been described as the most important religious event of the twentieth century.

Alberigo's first scholarly venture was not, however, about Vatican II, but about Italian bishops at the Council of Trent, the subject of his doctoral dissertation. With the book on Trent hardly published (1959), he was drawn into the circle of Cardinal Giacomo Lercaro, the Archbishop of Bologna, who would be a leading figure at Vatican II, and of Giuseppe Dossetti, a theologian close to the cardinal. Thus, once the Council got under way, Alberigo had an insider's vantage point as the event unfolded. His familiarly with Trent was not wasted, for it gave him a historical foil against which to view the new council. Ever since the 1960s, therefore, Giuseppe Alberigo has with his many publications taken the lead among historians in trying to set the Second Vatican Council into historical perspective and thus aid in its interpretation.

Despite all that has been written about Vatican II, its interpretation continues to vex historians, theologians, and the ecclesiastical establishment, who in that regard sometimes find themselves at odds with one another. Vatican II was a "meeting" like no other, vast in its proportions and wide-ranging in its scope. We should not be surprised that interpretations have emerged that seem almost to contradict one another and that are not always innocent of agenda. At this moment they fall into two main camps—those that insist the Council did not do much more than reaffirm the perennial faith of the Church and those that insist it did (or wanted to do) something more. Although Alberigo underscores the fundamental continuity of Vatican II with the Catholic tradition, he stands with excellent credentials in the latter camp.

The Council ended forty years ago. The main protagonists are gone from the scene, and even the basic contours of what happened are fading from the collective memory of Catholics around the world. For younger generations Vatican II can sound as remote as Trent and just as unfamiliar—one student defined it as "the pope's summer residence." It is for that reason Alberigo wrote this "brief history." In it he aims to provide a concise and reader-friendly overview of the story for those not intrepid enough to tackle the five volumes. He makes the account particularly engaging by including some personal reminiscences. There is no book like it in English. It fills a gap and should find a wide and appreciative readership.

Preface

Toward the end of the 1950s, shortly after I had turned thirty years old, I found myself involved in an unexpected adventure. Amid the general excitement created by his recent election, Pope John XXIII had announced the convening of a new council. I would have considered this simply a matter for clerics had I not been studying another council for a few years, the one held in Trent during the 1500s. I therefore had a professional interest in the new council, which prompted me to give it more attention than an average lay Catholic otherwise might, especially a married man with a daughter just a few years old.

In addition to this, I had been an assistant to Giuseppe Dossetti, a university professor who had become a priest, and I was still his close collaborator at an institute for research in religious studies in Bologna. This institute was connected to the city's archbishop, Cardinal Giacomo Lercaro, who would play a part in the upcoming Council.

But I also had a vital interest in the renewal of the Church and Christian life simply as a believer. I was a witness to the decline, and aging of Christianity (as evidenced in issues that ranged from the Latin Mass to the tendency to see the laity as inferior to the clergy) and the difficulty the Church had in reaching ordinary people. Could a council bring Catholicism out of an immobility that had seemed overwhelming and suffocating during the last years (from 1950 onward) of the pontificate of Pius XII?

The fact is that within a few weeks my life was turned upside down by the tasks that the prospect of this new council created. What could a small group of young students do? First of all, we began working on a book that would make it easier to consult the decisions made during previous councils. Under the invaluable leadership of Giuseppe Dossetti and the greatest intellectual authority on the councils at the time, the German scholar Hubert Jedin, I worked with other young "apprentices" on this process of compilation. We presented the book to the new pope at the beginning of October 1962, a few days before the opening of the new council.[1]

I was also involved in promoting a series of television spots on the previous Councils intended for the general public. Finally, as work at the Second Vatican Council was about to begin, we began to make contact with European theological faculties, study centers, and individuals interested in the upcoming assembly and the problems related to it. Italian Catholicism tended to be a bit too closed up within itself. At that time I was not an ecumenist, either in the sense of having an active commitment to the movement to bring Christian Churches closer together, or in the sense of being a student of the problems related to the divisions and relationships among Christians of various traditions. My first contact with the world of ecumenism came in 1960, when Benedictine Father Jean Leclerq, a great scholar of medieval monastic theology, and Hubert Jedin, the guide for my studies on the Council of Trent, got me an invitation to a session of the Catholic Conference for Ecumenical Questions, which was to be held that year in the Italian town of Gazzada, in the Varese region.

As a typical Italian Catholic, I was almost a teetotaler when it came to ecumenism. Even during my studies in Germany I came into contact only with Catholic circles. Giuseppe Dossetti's encouragement to consider the importance of the Eastern Christian tradition was valuable to me, since it broke through my almost exclusively Catholic horizon of experience and studies. Just a couple of years earlier Delio Cantimori, the great historian of heresies and heretics whom I had assisted at the University of Florence, had suggested to me that I prepare an anthology of the writings of the great protagonists of the Protestant Reformation for a short series of books to be produced by the Garzanti publishing house. This was my opportunity to plunge into a universe as unfamiliar to me as it was fascinating.

Participating in the Catholic Conference for Ecumenical Questions in September of 1960 was an introduction to the problems of Christian division. Attending were men like Cardinals Augustin Bea and Jan Willebrands, Bernard Alfrink, Olivier Rousseau, Pierre Duprey, Emanuel Lanne, Ives Congar, Hans Küng, and Charles Moeller, all of the eminent Catholic theologians dedicated to a renewal of Rome's stance toward the other Christian communities.

It was only later that I understood the full impact of John XXIII's decision, just a few months earlier (June 5, 1960), to include a Secretariat for Christian Unity among the preparatory commissions for Vatican II. This practically conferred an official status on our conference, which was destined to play a crucial part in both the preparation and the unfolding of the Council.

Participating in later sessions of the conference (Strasbourg, 1961; Gazzada, 1962 and 1963) helped me to orient myself within the general context of inter-Christian discussion. I was also helped by the friendships I quickly struck with various members of the conference (and also, by that time, with members of the secretariat), some of whom had given lectures at the institute in Bologna during the years of preparation for the Council. The widespread sense of anticipation at the prospects opened up by the pope's convening of the Council was fertile ground for new interaction and unexpected collaboration among the members of the small Bologna group. It may not have been a carefully planned process, but it was certainly timely and productive.

Then, in October 1962, the many participants in the Council assembly began meeting at St, Peter's in Rome, and Cardinal Lercaro, with Dossetti as his theological consultant, quickly became one of the leaders. Because I worked with both of them, I began to make regular trips from Bologna to Rome.

This fascinating and unforeseen development captured my interest and made a profound impact on me, widening my spiritual and cultural horizons. It put me into contact with all the major facets of the questions facing Christianity, and even though I was still an "outsider," it showed me the collegial dimension of the Church's life, expressed as a familial bond, not as the ties of a "business" organization. Day after day I learned the importance of how a large assembly is regulated, and the unimaginable impact this has on the work that it produces. The order in which the addresses were given, the length of the addresses themselves, and the language employed all had the effect of making the Council work better or worse. I saw in person how a commission of a few dozen persons can have a decisive influence on a Council of more than two thousand participants. I witnessed the forging of a conciliar consciousness among hundreds of bishops who until then had been accustomed to a profound individualism. Many of them underwent this experience willingly, recognizing that many others shared their problems and aspirations. But a few of them were afraid that they would be induced to compromise "tradition," the thought and practice of the past, and closed themselves off in a defensive attitude. I also saw hundreds of bishops of all different language and age groups, from very different social situations and backgrounds, attest to the need for renewal. Rather than points of division, their differences were shown to be complementary.

Except for the work of a limited number of specialists, the problems that the Council gradually faced were new, not in terms of their general schemata—the Bible, the liturgy, the Church, religious liberty, peace, and so forth—but in terms of the new perspective offered by theoretical and practical developments within the renewal movements of the first half of the twentieth century and because of the approach suggested by John XXIII. It was extremely interesting to accompany (though always from the outside of St, Peter's) the various successive phases of the Council's work, becoming familiar with extraordinarily interesting personalities and their points of view. It all contributed to a deeper understanding of many questions and created many memories.

Breaking free from old habits, questioning and transcending fixed attitudes, challenging oneself with "different" persons and convictions became a daily commitment. These moments almost always happened spontaneously and had to be reconciled with the need for intellectual rigor and with solid personal integrity. Such intense common activity meant fostering hope, finding disappointment, and experiencing success in deep communion with many others, beginning with my wife, Angelina, my constant participant in all this, who kept a valuable diary of those extraordinary years. Well after the conclusion of the Council, which met from 1962 to 1965, my firm belief in its importance led me to begin an initiative to compile a history of that event. So a few dozen scholars from all over the world worked from 1988 to 2000 to collect thousands of documents and to write and publish a five-volume *History of Vatican Council II*.[2] Many other books were published on the studies that went into the preparation of this history, and they give a more complete analysis of particular aspects.

This was an exhilarating endeavor in its own right and was well received in the various languages in which it was published—apart from Italian, there were versions in English, German, French, Spanish, Portuguese, and Russian. But now that I am almost eighty years old, and the work is done, I ask myself: What do my children know? What do my nephews and nieces and all that generation know about this adventure that took place half a century ago? The history of the Council may well be documented and analyzed in those great volumes totaling almost three thousand pages, but this question prompted me to try to write that history in a more accessible form for people who were not yet born when Vatican II was taking place, but who look upon a Catholicism and, indeed, a Christian movement as a whole, that has been deeply changed by the Second Vatican Council. The intense, relentless acceleration of events, which has increased even more after the passage from the second to the third millennium, threatens to marginalize historical memory, setting it aside as if it were a precious but unnecessary object. Even great events that have made a profound impact on the life and future of much of humanity quickly seem to grow so distant that they can be safely ignored.

The great conciliar assemblies make up the backbone of Christian history. The councils have constituted crucial moments during the historical journey of churches and believers, although sometimes their importance has taken centuries to be felt. In a way that goes beyond or even defies logic, those few councils that have been able to capture the central aspects of the Christian message have been the object of the close attention and participation of millions of "ordinary" believers who felt the charismatic influence of the assembly.

An understanding of what took place at them offers a unique and fundamental contribution to human knowledge. Forty years after the conclusion of the conciliar assembly that met in Rome, I wonder what is known today of the Council, its development, and its significance. The enthusiasm that characterized the anticipation and celebration of Vatican II has been extinguished. The generation of the participants is disappearing; even the "traditionalists" lead by dissident French bishop Marcel Lefebvre have seen the flame of their rejection of the Council go up in smoke. It is clear that the social context has changed profoundly since then, and a significant part of this change is due to the effects of the Council itself and the processes it set in motion.

Immediately after the conclusion of the Council's work, attention was focused on commenting upon the numerous official documents that had been produced. Vatican II was thus understood, to a certain extent, in the abstract, as if it were merely an abundant, even excessive, collection of documents—nothing but words. But at a distance of forty years, it figures as an event that—in spite of its limitations and shortcomings—has brought to modern life the hope and optimism of the gospel.

The Council did not intend to produce a new doctrinal *summa* (as John XXIII said, "a council was not necessary for this") or to respond to all problems. What characterized Vatican II was a sense of the duty of renewal, a thirst for understanding, a willingness to confront history, and a concern for all people as brothers and sisters. This is why priority should be given to the phenomenon of the Council itself as an event that assembled a deliberating body of more than two thousand bishops. The same is true of its decisions, which are to be interpreted not as cold, abstract norms but as an expression and continuation of the event itself.

So it is worthwhile to try to make Vatican II accessible for those who did not have the astonishing good fortune to experience it. This does not mean relegating it to the past, but rather proposing to the new generations that they use this book as a means of coming to a correct understanding of the Council's significance, and why this is still relevant. The day-to-day work of the Council lasted through 168 assemblies, adding up to just under a thousand hours, without counting the work of the commissions and groups. Reconstructing and depicting not only the complex development of this work, but also the spirit and dynamism that characterized the assembly, means placing this activity in the context of the growing awareness of the assembly and its various components. Also not to be lost from view are the relationships of exchange and encounter between the environment within the Council and the external context—that of Rome, and above all, that of the rest of the world.

It is obvious that the history of Vatican II can be reconstructed only on the basis of a critical analysis of the sources, of all the surviving documentation: oral and written, official and informal, collective and individual, internal and external. What a mountain! The question to be answered is not simply, How were the decisions of Vatican II approved? but above all, How did Vatican II take place on a practical level, and what was its significance?

From the celebration of Mass in the native language to the way of expressing the traditional faith, to how the Christian life is lived, the transformations Vatican II applied to Catholicism—and, indirectly, to the other Christian Churches as well—were so profound that it is difficult for the younger generations to understand their impact without adequate instruction. One could say the same thing in regard to the influence of both the Council and the pontificate of John XXIII on the attitudes of Catholics, and even of the Church itself, toward society and politics. Even before the crisis and collapse of the major ideologies, culminating in the collapse of the Berlin Wall in 1989 and in the disintegration of the USSR, Pope John XXIII and the Council had led Catholicism out of its sometimes suffocating affinity for the Western sociopolitical system under the hegemony of the United States. This meant the advent of a new stance toward the vast populations of the East. It also meant the severing of compromising entanglements, the end of the coalitions that the Church had formed with political parties such as Italy's Christian Democrats or France's Popular Republican Movement. The anxious mistrust of Catholics toward modernity was beginning to be superseded, although nostalgia for it would persist. With some awkwardness and considerable effort, a friendlier attitude was adopted toward humanity and its accomplishments.

Acknowledgments

I must acknowledge once again that throughout writing this book, I enjoyed the precious, indispensable assistance of Angelina Nicora, my spouse and the inseparable companion of my every adventure, as well as the able assistance of younger friends and colleagues, who patiently read drafts and suggested ways to improve its readability. This, too, is an act of solidarity in the communal spirit of the Council.

Catholic News Service

On June 5, 1960, Pope John XXIII issued the Motu Proprio (a document prepared "on his own initiative") *Superno Dei nutu*, which set up the preparatory commissions for Vatican II.

1

The Proclamation of the Council
(1959–1962)

A Surprise Announcement

"Standing before you I tremble somewhat with emotion but am humbly resolute in my purpose to proclaim a twofold celebration: a diocesan synod for the city of Rome, and a general Council for the universal Church." With these words, on January 25, 1959, less than ninety days after his election as the successor to Pius XII, Pope John XXIII announced his decision to convene a new council during a speech to a small group of cardinals gathered in the Roman basilica of St. Paul's Outside the Walls for the concluding liturgy of the week of prayer for Christian unity.[1] The pope added that the synod and council "would fortunately lead to the long-desired updating of the Code of Canon Law."

These were for him "the highest forms of apostolic activity that these three months of contact with the ecclesiastical atmosphere in Rome have suggested" and were announced with no intention other than that of "fostering the good of souls and bringing the new pontificate into clear and definite correspondence with the spiritual needs of the present day." It was, the pope continued, "a decisive resolution to recall some ancient ways of affirming doctrine and setting prudent guidelines for ecclesiastical discipline, which have produced extraordinarily rich fruit during times of renewal in the Church's history."

So this was a firmly held conviction, which John XXIII had developed by thinking about how effective other Councils had been for the renewal of the Church. The pope also affirmed that "the celebration of the ecumenical Council is not only intended for the edification of the Christian people, it is also an invitation to the separated communities in the quest for unity, which joins so many souls from every quarter of the world."

The conclave had elected Cardinal Angelo Roncalli, Bishop of Venice, as pope on October 28, 1958, in the context of a transitional pontificate, one that would be brief and would help to heal, through its tranquility, the

1

traumas of the long and dramatic reign of Pius XII. Certainly no one expected any overwhelming surprises from a pope nearly eighty years old, far less a surprise of such magnitude. For his part, John XXIII left no doubt about the definitive character of his decision to convene a council. He even showed that he was fully aware of the extraordinary nature of what he was doing, of this action undertaken as an exercise of papal primacy, requiring no participation from anyone else. It is no accident that the pope spoke of his "decisive resolution" and later remarked in his *Journal of a Soul* that "the ecumenical Council was entirely the initiative" of the pope.[2]

His announcement was unexpected and surprising for almost all sectors of the Church, which were dominated by the climate of the Cold War between the Soviet bloc and the Western bloc and satisfied with a Catholicism unyielding in its certainties. But the pope had spoken about "times of renewal." He believed, in fact, that the Church was on the threshold of an historical juncture of extraordinary intensity, in which it was necessary

> to specify and distinguish between what belongs to the realm of sacred principles and the perennial gospel, and what changes with the passing of time . . . We are entering a period that might be called one of universal mission . . . and we need to make our own the admonition of Jesus to recognize the "signs of the times" . . . and to discern amid such great darkness the many indications that give good cause for hope.[3]

But objectively, the relationship between the two blocs was always on the point of erupting into conflict: from the Korean War (1950) to the construction of the Berlin Wall (1961) to the nuclear missile crisis in Cuba (1962), the world seemed to have backed itself into a corner. It is true that the young president elected in November of 1960 in the United States—John F. Kennedy, a Catholic—aroused enthusiasm and opened up the prospects for renewal, but it is difficult to know how significant this was for the decision of the elderly pope.

In the areas characterized by a strong Christian presence, in the Northern Hemisphere, there was a widespread conviction that the churches had no choice but to support the anti-communist efforts of the Western bloc. But this was offset by a growing sense of disquiet nourished by the conviction that the centuries-old reciprocal support between political institutions and churches was in definitive decline. The modern version of Christendom seemed less and less a relevant and convincing model.

To many, the pope's age itself seemed contradictory in terms of a complex project that would take a long time to implement. Some, like French theologian Congar, maintained that different problems were in different phases of maturation and that, "from the theological point of view, above all in regard to the unity of the Christian Churches, it seemed that the Council was being held twenty years too soon."[4]

But something new had been happening in Catholicism, something that had been under way for a long while. Because of it, many ideas were changing, though it would still be a number of years before the emergence of bishops guided by ideas grounded in the Bible and tradition, and by a missionary and pastoral consciousness. Many, however, had made strides in their own understanding, and the very proclamation of the Council, with its ecumenical perspective, together with the more humane and Christian atmosphere of John XXIII's pontificate, promised to accelerate the process of renewal.

What was the significance of the announcement on January 25? Was one to expect the conclusion of the Rome council interrupted way back in 1870 by the conflict between France and Prussia? Would it be an occasion to reaffirm Roman Catholicism's understanding of itself, in substantial continuity with the almost supernaturally aloof personality of Pope Pius XII? Or was there room for something different? And, if so, what would the Council be able to do? The enthusiasm with which public opinion had greeted the announcement had nothing to do with these questions, but at the same time it shed light on an unsuspected reservoir of readiness and longing.

Who was this pope who, less than one hundred days after his election, called the Church to council from the four corners of the earth, launching the Roman Church into an adventure so daunting that the very prospect of it had made his predecessors turn aside? Born on November 25, 1881, into an extended family of sharecroppers in Sotto il Monte (in the province of Bergamo), Angelo Giuseppe Roncalli received a traditional upbringing. His family environment, with many children and scant economic means, was characterized by a robust sense of rural piety. "May our work cry aloud to the clergy and to all the people, the work by which we desire to 'prepare for the Lord a perfect people, make straight his paths, that the crooked ways be made straight, and the rough ways become smooth, that everyone may see the salvation of God.'"

This is how Roncalli—after his surprising choice of the name John— summarized the aims of his pontificate on October 28, 1958. A few days later, on the occasion of his coronation, he emphasized his commitment to being a good pastor, according to the description in the tenth chapter of the gospel of John, adding that "the other human qualities—knowledge, shrewdness, diplomatic tact, organizational abilities—can help the pope to carry out his office, but they can in no way substitute for his task as a pastor."

The Church was like a household for Roncalli, and the study of history had always fascinated him, so he had considered with some interest the significant role that the councils of earlier centuries had played in the life of the Christian community. This interest was, however, unusual in the general intellectual context of the Italian clergy at the time. He might have been more directly influenced to think of the opportunity for a new council by the intellectual currents circulating through the Christian world during the entire first half of the twentieth century. These ranged from the projects of the Eastern Orthodox Churches to the proposals favored by Pius XI and Pius XII to reconvene and conclude the Vatican council suspended in 1870. Roncalli, however, was not himself involved in these projects.

The turning point came with the awareness, conferred on him by his election to the papacy, that he was in a position of singular responsibility. On January 20, the "rather hesitant and uncertain" pope had informed secretary of state Cardinal Tardini, for the sake of protocol, of his "program for the pontificate: a Roman synod, an ecumenical Council, and the updating of the Code of Canon Law, assuming a full consensus and mandate."[5]

The convocation of the new council was essentially the fruit of one of the pope's personal convictions, which had long been growing within him. It was reinforced by other people, and finally, it became an authoritative and irrevocable decision within three months of his election to the pontificate.

The announcement of January 25 was irreversible; in the following months and years, Catholicism, the other Christian traditions, and even the secular world would have to come to terms with Roncalli's decision. The Catholic Church had entered a new and unforeseen phase of its history. Previously known as an element of continuity and identity for Western society, the Roman papacy began to provide an impulse toward change and renewal, even of society itself.

An Unexpected Response

The proclamation of the Council was greeted by a wide response from very different social and cultural circles, far beyond Roman Catholicism's ordinary domain of Western Europe and North America. This was one of the first indications of the universal impact that John XXIII's papacy and the Council would have. It is almost impossible to get an overall view of the first reactions and comments sparked by the announcement. The news spread all over the world in just a few hours, arousing attention, interest, and expectations with such a range of both fundamental and subtle differences that even the most accurate account cannot fully document them. The immediate general impression was that a profound change was taking place in the heart of Catholicism; everyone had a different idea of which outcomes and developments were most important, but what is really striking is the hope and expectation created in so many circles

In view of this climate it is astonishing that *L'Osservatore Romano*, the Vatican's newspaper, published only the press release from the secretariat of state, and that *La Civiltà Cattolica*—the Jesuits' authoritative biweekly magazine—completely ignored the announcement during the first quarter of 1959, apart from reproducing that same meager press release in its news summary. The first sign of interest appeared in the edition of April 25, 1959, with a collection of comments on the announcement taken from the press. But the magazine did not dedicate a full article to the announcement during the whole of 1959.

According to a letter sent to Milan Archbishop Montini from an authoritative observer, Giuseppe De Luca: "The Rome that you know and were exiled from [by Pius XII's decision to send Montini to Milan] shows no sign of changing, even though it seemed that it must sooner or later. After their initial fright, the old buzzards are coming back. Slowly, but they're coming back. And they are coming with a thirst for new carnage and fresh revenge. That macabre circle is tightening around the *carum caput* [John XXIII]. Without a doubt, they are back."[6]

It was bitterly clear that an "institutional isolation" would characterize the pontificate of John XXIII, when the pope's institutional collaborators, and above all the congregations of the Curia, would create opposition to the pope's intentions, leaving him alone. John XXIII's isolation is well documented in a retrospective letter by Italian Benedictine Fr. Cipriano Vagaggini, who from firsthand experience pointed out

a few details that might be able to confirm what is known from other sources.

1. I recall that when the first meeting of consultants for the Liturgical Commission was held at the Vatican, Fr. Bugnini, the commission's secretary, introduced us to Archbishop Felici, secretary for the Council. Among the other things he said, Archbishop Felici told us something I have never forgotten. He said that when Pope John announced the Council, the Roman Curia asked that the topics for discussion be determined by sending a detailed questionnaire to the bishops, theologians, etc., asking them what they thought about the questions posed. This was, naturally, a way of drastically limiting from the outset the questions that could be considered at the Council. Archbishop Felici told us that Pope John did not permit this, but said that the parties concerned must simply be asked what were, in their judgment, the questions that should be considered at the Council. This is, in fact, what was done.

According to Archbishop Felici, the Roman Curia also asked Pope John that the head of each pre-conciliar and conciliar commission be the prefect of the corresponding Roman dicastery. For example, the prefect of the Holy Office would head the commission on doctrine, the prefect of the Congregation of Rites would head the commission on the liturgy, etc. The secretary of each of these commissions would also be the secretary of the corresponding dicastery. This was an attempt to put the entire organizational structure into the hands of the

Roman Curia. Archbishop Felici told us that Pope John gave his permission that the prefect of the individual commissions be the prefect of the respective Roman dicastery, but he wanted the commission secretaries to be selected from outside of the Roman Curia. And that is what took place.

2. After Pope John had proclaimed the Council at St. Paul's Outside the Walls, a secretary of one of the cardinals (perhaps Cardinal Fietta) told me the following. A few days before the meeting, the cardinals had been notified that the pope would be going to St. Paul's, and they were asked to be present because the pope was going to speak to the cardinals and the monks in the monastery's chapter room, and he had important things to say. The secretary brought this to the cardinal's attention and encouraged him to attend. The cardinal replied: "What sort of important thing could he say on such an occasion? He will give an exhortation to the monks, nothing more." He didn't go, and of course he was chagrined when he heard about the announcement of Vatican Council II. This episode proves that at least a large part of the Roman Curia did not know about the pope's intentions before the official proclamation. If it had been known, it would have spread immediately throughout the Curia.

3. One more episode demonstrates that even the most competent circles of the Curia knew nothing about the pope's intention to convene a council. I was at the pontifical college of Sant' Anselmo when it happened. The day after the official announcement, one of my confreres, who was a consultant for the Holy Office and worked rather frequently at the Curia, went over to that congregation. That evening when he returned he was utterly amazed and excited, saying that everyone at the congregation was agitated and couldn't understand how a pope could suddenly announce a council without first consulting the appropriate sections of the Curia and preparing for what was not at all an easy task. The moral of the story is that when Pope John announced Vatican Council II, not even the congregation of the Holy Office was aware of what was happening.

These are minor details, but they demonstrate how it was Pope John personally who wanted to call the Council; how the Roman Curia, or at least much of it, was unaware of this; and how the Curia then tried to take control of Council proceedings, but without support from Pope John.[7]

The pope's initiative may have received public appreciation from the bishops rather slowly, but it found a particularly ready reception and a sympathetic attitude among the sectors that had been hoping for, conceiving, and experimenting with the liturgical, biblical, and ecumenical renewal of Catholicism. The inner circles of these movements likewise quickly perceived in the new pope a welcoming and fully sympathetic attitude, in stark contrast with the cold and somewhat mistrustful attitude of his predecessor. While it is relatively easy to find out the reactions of the most prominent groups, it is almost impossible to make an account of all the comments made through the most disparate means of communication, from diocesan and parish newspapers to radio stations and television networks.

The announcement did not escape the vigilant attention of the mayor of Florence, Giovanni La Pira, who called it an event "of immense supernatural and historical significance." A few months later he noted that "the Council itself is the essential 'political' event upon which depend peace among peoples and their future political, social, cultural, and religious organization."[8]

An "Ecumenical" Council?

John XXIII's announcement was a turning point in the laborious quest for Christian unity, providing an unforeseen catalyst. That the pope should be the one to take the initiative for unity among the churches and to outline the process in terms of cooperation toward creating "a single flock,"[9] and no longer in terms of returning to the past, was unexpected almost to the point of being unbelievable. It provoked disparate reactions and required a complete rethinking of ecumenical strategy.

Even in relation to this aspect of the announcement, before the reactions of the "qualified experts" and their circles, there was a manifestation of interest from many non-Catholic Christians who intuitively saw in John XXIII a fraternal attitude rather than the old hostility. Toward the end of March 1959 the representative of the Orthodox Patriarch of Constantinople at the World Council of Churches, Metropolitan Iakovos of Malta, arrived in Rome. Pope John received him as a special representative of Ecumenical Patriarch Athenagoras, who had responded immediately to the pope's message of January 1, 1959.[10] There was, moreover, a very lively interest in the prospects for the Council on the part of the other Orthodox Churches. A Greek newspaper emphasized early on that "we now find ourselves facing a new situation." The Coptic Orthodox Church and the Patriarchate of Antioch also expressed their attentive consideration of the pope's initiative.

The most rapid reaction to the announcement came from the Geneva headquarters of the World Council of Churches—a consortium of the Christian Churches removed from Rome, the "separated brothers and sisters"—through the initiative of Willem A. Visser 't Hooft, a pastor of the Dutch Reformed Church and secretary general of the WCC. As early as January 27 Visser 't Hooft expressed a "very particular interest" in John XXIII's gesture toward Christian unity; two weeks later the executive commission of the WCC made this declaration its own. The Geneva group was not only attentive to the new vibrations emanating from Rome, but it also had a lively interest in keeping Rome from monopolizing a new ecumenical phase. It asked itself what the meaning of the expression *ecumenical council* might be; that is, whether it implied the direct participation of other Christian Churches or simply an invitation to a common search for unity.

The Anglican Archbishop of Canterbury took the initiative of sending a cleric, I. Rea, with a letter for John XXIII; this was a prelude to the archbishop's consequent visit to Rome. But the announcement from Rome also provoked uncertainty and reservations, which were based upon a lack of trust toward the Catholic Church and its usual dogmatic and institutional positions. It was thought crucial that any excessively easy agreement be avoided, because in the enthusiastic climate of a revived emphasis on harmony at all costs, this might leave unresolved the problems that needed to be faced with sincerity and realism.

A few months after the first announcement of the Council, it became clear that while the pope's effort to imbue the Council itself with a special significance for inter-Christian relations had been very well received by public opinion, it was coming up against serious obstacles, both in Rome and in the most authoritative non-Catholic circles, from the World Council of Churches in Geneva to the Greek Orthodox patriarchates. Some Catholics had trouble overcoming the age-old hostilities toward the "heretics" (Protestants) and the "schismatics" (Eastern Orthodox), and others feared that the pope's initiative concealed intentions of domination and pointed toward the absorption of other Christians into the Roman Church.

It is surprising that in spite of the overwhelming secularization—at least in the West—that made the very notion of a council difficult to grasp, John XXIII's announcement unleashed a great outburst of attention, interest, and above all, anticipation from public opinion. The people—believers and nonbelievers, Catholics and non-Catholics—instinctively understood that the elderly pope's initiative was a highly significant act and saw in it a sign of hope, a sign of confidence in the future and in the prospects for renewal. They also showed a willingness—unsophisticated, perhaps, but authentic—to become involved, a willingness that they felt was welcomed. Almost without any assistance, the pope's initiative reached millions of people and convinced them of their own potential for liberation and innovation. The Cold War climate between the ideologically opposed capitalist and communist blocs had introduced habits of watching over and even suppressing manifestations of spontaneity. But on this occasion, the control mechanisms were overwhelmed by a spontaneous and enthusiastic response to the announcement, which promised liberation from ideological barriers and unleashed new hope.

One interesting reverberation of the January 25 announcement can be seen in the reports made from Rome by the diplomatic representatives accredited to the Holy See or to the Italian republic. Some of them, like those at the U.S. embassy, were preoccupied with the uncertain fate of the

Italian government and practically ignored the announcement. But a number of others, like those at the embassy of the federal republic of Germany, began asking what the practical effects of these ecumenical aspirations would be. The highest Soviet officials in Moscow were raising some rather sophisticated questions.[11]

What Kind of Council?

Not even the full text of the January 25 announcement responded to the many questions that it raised. The information on the nature of the upcoming council was very sparse and left a lot of room for the most disparate hypotheses and flights of fancy. It is also true that John XXIII did not give birth to a fully formed council, like Minerva springing from the brain of Jupiter. Its aims and nature were gradually sketched out, tested, and deepened in terms of their weight and implications as the pope continued to reflect upon them. His thought was also affected by the response and criticism from the Church and from other Christians, by the development of world events, and finally by the beginning of preparations for the Council itself.

During the two months following the announcement, debate on the upcoming Council was undertaken with some difficulty. It seemed that no one really knew what to say. Was it perhaps that no one dared to express points of view that the pope might not like? Or was there still some hope that the idea would simply fade away? Was this a matter of real disorientation over an unforeseen eventuality? People who had thought they were imprisoned in a rigid system of Church life and theological reflection now found that they were alive and free, but it was difficult for them to regain the exercise of that liberty. Nevertheless, something was beginning to happen.

It was only at the end of April 1959 that Pope John formulated the fundamental aim of the Council: to increase Christians' commitment to their faith, "to make more room for charity . . . with clarity of thought and greatness of heart."[12] Having established that, he did not hesitate to characterize the upcoming Council in absolutely traditional terms. That is, it would be a free and responsible council of bishops, and thus it would be able to conduct effective deliberation—but it would do so with the *sui generis* participation of representatives from the non-Catholic Christian Churches.

This created the necessity of continually distinguishing between the Council and the Curia. The Curia was responsible for the daily business and ordinary management of Church life, and this had to be distinguished clearly from the Council and preparations for it. This was another means of emphasizing the pope's intention that the Council be situated in a context outside of the ordinary and that the powerful structure of the Curia be prevented from taking control of it. The pope wanted a council that would mark the end of an era; a council, that is, that would usher the Church out of the post-Tridentine era, and to a certain extent out of the centuries-old Constantinian phase, and into a new phase of witness and proclamation. The major permanent elements of tradition judged most suitable would be enlisted to nourish and guarantee fidelity to the gospel during such an arduous transition.

With the approach of the Feast of Pentecost—the liturgical commemoration of the descent of the Holy Spirit upon the apostles—John XXIII began to refer to the Council as a "new Pentecost."[13] The image of a new Pentecost would come to be habitually associated with the conciliar assembly, to the point of being included in the pope's prayer for the Council, in which he asked the Holy Spirit to renew "your wonders in our own age, as in a new Pentecost." Nevertheless,

> little by little, the hopes raised by the proclamation of the Council were obscured as though by a thin layer of ashes. There was a long silence, a sort of blackout, interrupted only occasionally by some cheerful statement from the pope. But these declarations were rather vague, and seemed to retreat from the stance of the original announcement. This was widely noticed, even though the pope himself declared publicly that his intentions had not changed.[14]

This note from the middle of 1959 by French Dominican theologian Congar is a good example of the perception and assessment of the situation in Rome during those months. Thus the decision to form a "pre-preparatory commission" for the Council, made public on May 17, 1959, came as a surprise. Plans for the Council had not been abandoned, after all. This was all the more important in that preparations had already begun for the synod of the Diocese of Rome, which had been announced together with the Council.

Who Was Involved in the Council Preparations? (1959–1960)

A restricted initial group responsible for preparing for the Council had been formed as early as February 6, 1959. Using as a model the preparations for the Vatican Council of 1870, this was made up of a restricted commission of cardinals with a support staff of specialists in the areas of doctrine, canon law, Church discipline, and the separated churches. The papal declaration issued on Pentecost established the composition of the commission and determined its tasks.[15] Almost all of the ten members were Italians who worked in Rome, and all of the congregations of the Roman Curia had been guaranteed representation. The presidency was assigned to Cardinal Domenico Tardini, the secretary of state; the secretary of the commission was an obscure auditor of the Vatican tribunal (the Roman Rota), Pericle Felici. Not even the analogous commission named by Pius XII to prepare for a future council had been so completely monopolized by the Curia.

The group's task was to gather material that would permit the start of preparations for the Council's work. The commission was to delineate the topics to be considered at the Council and to formulate proposals for the composition of working bodies that would manage the real and proper preparation for the Council itself. The commission, which was labeled the Pre-preparatory Commission, wanted to prepare a questionnaire that would be sent to all bishops, soliciting their views; their responses would then be analyzed by this same commission. Their outline of likely topics for the Council's work included the priestly and lay ministries, the family, the nature of the Church, relations between Church and state, the adaptation of ecclesiastical organization to the needs of modern times, the missions, relations between bishops and religious, and social doctrine. Support also grew for the opinion that it would be helpful if the various congregations of the Curia would play some role in managing the topics of their expertise. What was entirely missing was an organic, overall vision of the Council's activity.

But the novelty in all this was found in the fact that John XXIII had entrusted responsibility for this phase to the secretariat of state and not to the feared—and sometimes hated—Supreme Congregation of the Holy Office (formerly the Inquisition). By doing this, he prevented the "supreme congregation" from enjoying a monopoly over the Council. This decision clearly showed the pope's preference that the Council not be prepared in the traditionally doctrinaire style and intransigent atmosphere of the Holy Office. It was a decision that entailed a great number of consequences and provoked many reactions.

The pope, moreover, by declining to entrust the preparation for the Council to a commission outside of the Curia, also performed an act of trust and delegation. This was inspired by his desire and hope to attain the Curia's loyalty in regard to the Council. And yet the Roman and Curial composition of the Pre-preparatory Commission was the object of a lively response, especially outside of Italy. Was the Council, then, entrusted to an exclusive group of high-level bureaucrats, the majority of whom were not even formally bishops? These reactions influenced the various phases of the commission's work, especially when it came to the question of consulting the bishops and the Roman Curia; the principle was established that all the bishops, not only some, should be consulted, in contrast with procedures under both Pius XI and Pius XII.

With the failure of the idea of consulting the bishops by means of a questionnaire, the pope invited everyone to indicate the problems and topics that the Council should consider. During the following months about two thousand responses came to the Vatican from all over the world.

The majority of these writings demonstrated surprise and disorientation. Rome was not issuing orders, but was asking for suggestions! Many hoped that the Council would occupy itself with topics of only modest importance; very few had wide horizons and were accustomed to taking bold points of view.

The pope's decision to begin a pre-preparatory phase thus retrieved the announcement of the Council made four months earlier from its condition of uncertainty and confirmed his intention to follow through with it. But some circles were counting on a period of delay that, given the pope's advanced age, might mean setting the Council aside definitively. So it came as a turning point all the more significant in this climate when on July 14, 1959, John XXIII wrote to Cardinal Tardini about the name for the Council; it would be called Vatican II. The pope thus affirmed unequivocally that this would be a new council, not a completion of Vatican I, which had been left unfinished in 1870. And because the Council would be new, its agenda would be entirely free and open. It would not be the continuation of a council convened and then interrupted in a historical context of conflict and pessimism (the pope as a prisoner in the Vatican). It would be a blank page in the centuries-old history of the councils.

The first six months of the time leading up to Vatican II seemed intended above all for putting an end to the surprise and disorientation occasioned by the announcement. The pope confirmed his decision and gradually unveiled how he saw the Council. The Roman Curia also turned an eye toward the matter, cherishing dreams of obtaining control. The Catholic bishops were shocked by the invitation to assume an active role at the level of the universal Church, and it would take some effort to create an atmosphere of inquiry after the long period of passivity experienced during the preceding pontificates. (Fr. Milani would shout, "Obedience is not a virtue anymore!")

The response from the bishops, an enormous amount of material, has received various interpretations. Some point to the later attitudes of the bishops at the Council and say that the first opinions they sent in were inspired by a preconciliar mentality and are devoid of value. Others see in them a somewhat colorless self-portrait of the Church on the eve of the Council. The sorting of the responses was undertaken at the beginning of September 1959 and concluded at the end of January 1960. The work involved was staggering; in order to manage it, an index had to be compiled, "An Analytical Synthesis of the Advice and Suggestions from the Bishops" (*Analyticus conspectus consiliorum et votorum quae ab episcopis et praelatis data sunt*). It divided the material into eighteen parts and was imposing in its own right; it came to more than fifteen hundred pages.

After this, the syntheses were broadly classified by geographical area, and between February 13 and April 1 John XXIII was familiarized with their contents. At last there was produced a brief "Final Synthesis of the Advice and Suggestions from the Most Reverend Bishops and Prelates of the Whole World for the Future Ecumenical Council." This concluded the work of the Pre-preparatory Commission. On the basis of this synthesis, the secretary of the Pre-preparatory Commission composed during July 1960 "Questions Posed to the Preparatory Commission of the Council" (*Quaestiones commissionibus praeparatoriis Concilii Oecumenici Vaticani II positae*). There were fifty-four topics divided into eleven categories.

The theological circles that had grasped most quickly the novelty of John XXIII's pontificate and his proclamation of the Council were engaged in putting the ideas into order. They were frequently dumbfounded at the idea that room for renewal had really been opened up. Non-Catholic Christians seemed to be divided between their initial good-natured anticipation and the cautiousness that followed. Can Rome change? they seemed to ask themselves, incredulous and perhaps mistrustful. In any case, plans for the Council had not been aborted, and a complex and contentious phase of preparation was under way.

The Official Preparations (1960–1962)

Preparing for an assembly composed of thousands of participants was a very complex task. On June 5, 1960, a central commission and ten commissions for the different thematic areas were named in Pope John's Motu Proprio *Superno Dei nutu*. The commissions were vested with the competencies of the Curial congregations and were headed by the cardinals who led the respective congregations.[16] The most striking exception to this institutional arrangement was the inclusion among the preparatory commissions (in addition to one on the apostolate of the laity—the activity of ordinary Christians for the spreading of the gospel) of the Secretariat for Christian Unity, which the pope had created a few weeks earlier at the suggestion of a German archbishop and Cardinal Bea.[17]

With some difficulty a series of nominations withdrew the composition of this apparatus from the complete monopoly of the Curia and the networks already established in Rome. This permitted the participation of bishops from all over the world, theologians from schools other than that of Rome, and even some of those who had been hit with sanctions under Pius XII. But it is undeniable that the Rome networks, which had the advantage of working on their own home territory, continued to exercise a predominant influence during this phase.

In the absence of a comprehensive vision, the preparatory work—which consisted of the selection of questions to be considered and the production of documents to be submitted for the approval of the Council—was scattered over countless topics, which were frequently of secondary importance. There was a prevailing tendency to piece together the various recommendations using the doctrinal and disciplinary teachings of the most recent popes, and especially those of Pius XII, in the conviction that the

Council would endow them with its solemn authority. It seemed, in fact, that the work of the Council would proceed rapidly, in just a few weeks, without any tension or tumultuous debates.

After a little more than two years of work based on the "Questions" of 1960, the preparatory body had produced more than seventy projects, many of them quite wordy and dedicated to the most disparate topics imaginable. John XXIII put an end to this phase on February 2, 1962, with his Motu Proprio "Concilium," in which he fixed the upcoming October 11 as the date for the Council assembly to begin its work. The formal convocation of the Council took place on December 25, 1961, with the Apostolic Constitution "Humanae Salutis." The silent opposition was disappointed once again.

In the meantime the features of the Council had begun to come into view, and three of these were especially prominent. First, this would not be a Council expressly dedicated to unity among the divided Christian traditions (Protestant, Anglican, and Orthodox), as rumor had had it and as the pope's expression "ecumenical council" had seemed to imply. Nevertheless, Pope John had repeatedly emphasized that the Council must signal a fundamental shift in the willingness of Catholics to participate in ecumenical efforts for unity among all the Christian Churches. Fostering this willingness would above all require the renewal of Catholicism itself. The Secretariat for Christian Unity instituted in 1960 was the linchpin of this approach.

A second characteristic involved the pastoral approach of the Council, which the pope affirmed each time he spoke of it. What did he mean? He seemed to mean that, rather than the classical pairing of doctrine and discipline, or faith and morals, used to indicate the topics that fell under Church teaching, he preferred an overall consideration of what was needed in the life of the Church, both within itself and in its relationship to society. This was a strictly evangelical attitude inspired by solidarity toward all and constantly motivated by the effort to make the Church reflect Christ, the good shepherd, in every one of its acts. It had the effect of discouraging the definition of new dogmas and the thunderous proclamation of new condemnations in the area of discipline. A fraternal approach would be sought instead, one inspired by the example of Jesus.

Finally, the third characteristic concerned the practical freedom of the Council, in which the bishops would be the real main characters, leaving behind the attitude of passivity that had characterized the Catholic episcopacy, especially after the definitions of the primacy and infallibility of the pope. This was in contrast, however, to the bishops' lack of good information about the preparatory work, which was covered with a shroud of secrecy and carried out using the Latin language.

While the official preparations were under way, interest in the Council was slowly growing through reflections, studies, and meetings taking place on many levels. Increasingly lively attention was being paid to the Council as a historic occasion for recovering the elements of a Christian experi-ence rooted in the life of the people, elements that had been marginalized by the imposing predominance of ecclesiastical institutions. Above all, it was an occasion for revitalizing the task of evangelization and witness. These spontaneous responses were not connected, but they were convergent, and they were full of dynamism, generosity, and expressive power—and were frequently underestimated or ignored by the official commissions.

It is extraordinary that those involved in the preparations, since they trusted in the representative character of the institutional apparatus, did not seek out opportunities to establish contact between the official prepa-ratory bodies and the spontaneous activity that the announcement had occasioned. This would have avoided many of the surprises that unsettled a large part of the Roman contingent, especially during the first weeks of the Council's activity.

One month before the start of the Council, on September 11, 1962, a radio message from the pope expressed his conviction that the Council had come "at the right moment," that is, at one of the "historic moments for the Church, in which it is ready to make a new leap toward the loftiest heights." The Council was called to be "a renewed face-to-face encounter with the risen Christ, the glorious and immortal king, and a continuation, or better, a more energetic revival of the response of the entire modern world to the word of the Lord." The pope emphasized how the "precious links in the chain of love" that has united all Christians for centuries "present themselves now to the attention of all who are not heedless of the new breezes being stirred up here and there by the plans for the Council, in anxious longing for fraternal reconciliation in the arms of our common ancient mother."

But the statement that found the widest and deepest response in pub-lic opinion was that "the Church presents itself to underdeveloped coun-tries as what it really is, and wants to be: the Church of all, and particu-larly of the poor." While the process of decolonization was intensifying in Africa and Asia, and many third-world bishops were preparing to par-ticipate in the Council on an equal footing with those of the rich world, John XXIII was affirming the Church's commitment to embodying the message of the gospel among these peoples as well, with special attention for the least advantaged (the "underdeveloped," as they were called back then).

Finally, during the summer—breaking the seal of silence that had ob-scured all of the preparatory work—the bishops were sent an initial group of seven schemata or "outlines" on the sources of revelation, the deposit of faith, the moral order, the liturgy, the family, social communications, and Church unity.[18] Many of the reactions the bishops sent to Rome expressed dissatisfaction, emphasizing the disparity between the perspectives indicated by the pope and the orientation of these schemata. Only the schema on the liturgy met with widespread agreement.

During those summer months the fear began to spread that the out-dated tendencies of the preparation were suffocating the Council. Would the bishops be able to respond to the plans prepared in Rome? Both Cardinal Suenens of Belgium and Cardinal Léger of Canada met with the pope to express this concern in no uncertain terms.

How the Assembly Worked

In the meantime the model of the First Vatican Council held one hundred years earlier was used to prepare the rules of order for the conciliar assembly.[19] Given the elevated number of members (more than two thousand) their geographical diversity, and their general lack of experience with assemblies, the working procedures they would be using were of enormous significance, and, as would soon become clear, would condition the functioning of the assembly to an unexpected degree. The rules of order provided for two levels of activity: that of the plenary assembly (general congregations) for the discussions, and that of the working groups (eleven commissions plus two administrative bodies) for the elaboration of the documents embodying the Council's decisions. The final step would be the approval of the decisions in the solemn sessions, the official sessions of the conciliar assembly in which the definitive vote would be conducted.

The work was to be directed by a Council of Presidents (of ten, later twelve, cardinals), assisted by a general secretary. Each commission was to be headed by a cardinal designated by the pope, who would also nominate eight bishops, one-third of the twenty-four members, while the other two-thirds—or sixteen bishops—would be elected by the Council. There were also provisions for the participation of experts—periti—who would carry out administrative and consultative functions but would not have the right to speak at the plenary sessions.

Since the spring of 1960 the German Jesuit Cardinal Bea had raised the question of inviting observers from the non-Catholic Christian Churches. There were no precedents for this. A number of centuries earlier the Greek-speaking Orthodox Church had been involved in the Councils of Lyons and Florence but as a full participant rather than an observer; at the Council of Trent the Protestants had participated for a short period of time, since the separation was already too deep at that point for more extensive involvement; on the occasion of Vatican I the Eastern Orthodox Christians and the Protestants had ignored Pius IX's clumsy invitation. But now the sophisticated efforts of the Secretariat for Christian Unity had led to the insertion of a chapter in the rules of order according to which observers from among the "separated Christians," after informing their respective communities, could participate in the solemn sessions and the general congregations (and eventually in the work of the commissions as well).

Moreover, the desire that the Catholic bishops of the countries behind the Iron Curtain (Poland, Hungary, Romania, Bulgaria, the Baltic states, Russia) also be free to participate in the Council gave John XXIII the idea of asking the Vatican's representative in Turkey to establish discreet contact with the Soviet ambassador. The aim of this was to convince the Soviet government of Moscow not to oppose the participation of these bishops at the Council. It was an innovative and courageous initiative, since there had been no relations between the Vatican and Moscow for decades, and an intransigent anti-communism reigned in Catholic circles. The initiative not only succeeded, it also unleashed a historical process of "thawing" between the West and the East, later known as Ostpolitik.

The plans submitted for examination at the Council were first of all discussed at the general congregations to decide what could and could not be proposed. If the voting that concluded this preliminary discussion was favorable, a chapter by chapter examination of the document was begun. During this phase the bishops—the "Council fathers"—could propose amendments (additions, modifications, cancellations) that were then validated by the competent commissions, which could accept them, integrating them into the text, or reject them. The revised text was returned to the general assembly for examination and was then voted upon, first by chapters, and then in its entirety. Voting would permit an affirmative response (*placet*), a negative one (*non placet*), or one of conditional approval (*placet iuxta modum*); a text would be approved when it had obtained a vote of consent from two-thirds of those present. Latin was the only language admitted, and an offer to set up a translation system was refused. Everything was kept secret.

The plenary sessions—always held in the morning—would begin with the celebration of the Mass and the enthronement of the Book of the Gospel, which symbolized the guiding presence of Christ, and would meet in the immense Vatican basilica of St. Peter. It was the only place that, once properly furnished, would be able to provide seats for the more than two thousand participants. The commissions, on the other hand, would work during the afternoons in different locations, sometimes even outside of Rome (especially during periods when the assembly was not meeting). Providing for the thousands of Council participants—not only the bishops, but also the official and unofficial experts, the observers, and the many journalists sent from around the world—had created serious logistical problems in Rome, producing an inconvenient dispersal that would be counteracted through the spontaneous creation of meeting points, such as the informal discussions held during long bus trips, which fostered the exchange of opinions.

In the meantime the Roman synod had been celebrated one year after its announcement, from January 24–31, 1960, in the cathedral of St. John Lateran. The formal decrees of this assembly of the clergy of the Diocese of

Rome were approved on June 28. It was the first diocesan synod of Rome in the entire modern era! The essential significance of the synod was that it revealed the pope's character as Bishop of Rome and the authentically diocesan nature of the Church of Rome. These were two obvious facts, but it had seemed that the Church had forgotten about them, since Rome was frequently seen as an extraterritorial reality in respect to the Church.

The synod itself ended in failure. It lacked a structure capable of understanding and channeling John XXIII's deepest intuitions. Its preparation and celebration were of a markedly clerical character, and it was never able to harness the evangelical power of the city. The diocese was unprepared and was bogged down in a centuries-old condition of fragmentation. It must be added that, for many, Rome, as the center of Christianity, could not be compared to any other diocese or subjected to normal pastoral procedures. On the other hand, leaving aside the synod itself, more than a decade later the Roman Church began to reap the benefits of the impulse toward renewal fostered by John XXIII. For his part, in spite of concerns that a negative assessment of the synod would reflect poorly on the plans for the Council—which is exactly what some were hoping—the pope did not conceal his own reservations, as can be gathered from the speech he gave to the Roman clergy on November 24, 1960. He recalled, with just a touch of irony, that imperfections had not been lacking "from the initial encounter on January 24 in our sacrosanct Lateran basilica, to the more solemn one on June 29 at the tomb of St. Peter. But we were able, with the Lord's help, to obtain a good result, even if in some ways it was not a perfect one."

Preparation for What Sort of Council?

The preparations for Vatican II were extravagant and excessive. Not only did they last longer than the celebration of the Council itself, but they were prominently characterized by an institutional approach. The pope was the supreme moderator, the Roman Curia was the chief agent, and the bishops and theologians—especially the European ones—gradually became involved to a considerable extent.

Reconstruction of the events of the pre-preparatory and preparatory phases on the basis of abundant published and unpublished documents has brought to light the complexity of this work, which absorbed considerable energy, beginning with the enormous volume of responses sent to Rome during the general consultation of 1959–60. John XXIII wanted to clear the way for a real and proper celebration of the Council in an atmosphere of complete freedom, and he repeatedly asserted that the preparations constituted an area of the Catholic Church's life distinctly different from the daily exercise of ordinary governance. It was a thinly veiled suggestion that the Curia avoid interfering.

Was it reasonable to expect that consultation with the bishops would result in proposals capable of realizing John XXIII's startling project? Or did the surprise that greeted the announcement make it less realistic to expect a significant response? It must also be recognized, however, that it would not have been possible to convene an assembly of more than two thousand participants without a prior phase of involvement and thorough preparations. The vision of a new Council, and not a completion of the interrupted Vatican I, was the guiding principle for the pope's project, and everyone needed some time just to get used to the idea itself.

What was the meaning of what the pope identified was to be the Council's dominant characteristic—the pastoral approach? This idea was for a long time trivialized and understood in the sense of focusing the Council on a nontheological, purely operational level—on "little shop-keeping details." It was only on the eve of the opening of the Council that progress was made toward solid acceptance of the pastoral approach in the sense of the subordination of every other aspect of the Church's life to the demanding image of Christ as the good shepherd.

Catholic News Service

On Christmas Day 1961 Pope John XXIII signed the document convoking Vatican II, saying he covened the Council so the Church could contribute positively to the solution of modern problems.

More than any other form of testimony, the years of preparation are themselves the most convincing documentation of the Church's lack of preparation for the commitment to participation and shared responsibility required by the celebration of a council, and of the condition of anguished immobility afflicting Catholicism. Almost without realizing it, Catholicism had drifted along a path of centralizing all decision-making in Rome, and, to an even greater extent, of concentrating this in the person of the pope. This situation was heading toward the creation of a monolithic structure. Experiencing Catholicism as the besieged fortress of truth was a position of apparent strength but substantial weakness. Any dynamic and vital impulse ran the risk of being looked upon with suspicion and deprived of the necessary room to express itself and grow.

While the management of the Council was quickly concentrated in institutional hands in Rome and shrouded in an almost impenetrable secrecy, parallel preparations were also taking place. These were carried out by countless anonymous participants from all parts, sustained and motivated by the deluge of public actions and declarations coming from John

XXIII. He had never stopped shaping the image of the Council as a universal summons to all Christians, though on different levels, to seek unity and renewal. It was above all this frequently anonymous, informal, widespread, spontaneous preparation that made it possible for the Council to be an event of efficacious renewal.

The liturgical movement had for decades criticized the passivity of the faithful—the spectators of a sacred drama—during liturgical celebrations and had argued for the need for the people's active participation in worship and the corollary necessity for the use of their mother tongues, since Latin was no longer understood by the laity, or even by the clergy. The movement for the promotion of the laity insisted upon an ever greater appreciation of the importance of the non-ordained in the heart of the Church.

For its part, the biblical movement brought back into view the centrality of the word of God, and at the same time, efforts for the renewal of theology appealed for a return to the sources (ressourcement). The ecumenical movement wanted to leave behind the era of Roman intransigence toward particular manifestations of unity. Finally, there was a widespread conviction that Catholicism needed to complete the definitions of the pope's prerogatives made in 1870 with others expressing the theological and sacramental nature of the bishop's office.

Some theologians, especially in the central-western region of Europe, understood the historic occasion that the Council represented. These were theologians like the Dominicans M.-D. Chenu and Ives Congar, and Edward Schillebeeckx, as well as German-speaking Jesuits such as Karl Rahner, and French-speaking Jesuits like Henri de Lubac, and the Swiss theologian Hans Küng. In addition to these there were centers of reflection that had been active for decades. like Le Saulchoir for the Dominicans, Fourvière for the Jesuits, and the theological faculties of Louvain, Tübingen, and Innsbruck. Their common denominator was a sense of urgency that Catholicism must emerge from the tired and sterile period of the Counter-Reformation.

Finally, from a sociological point of view, the preparations seem to have been concentrated in the hands of a restricted group composed exclusively of celibate males, culturally European and of a rather elevated average age. Although this group was imbued with the tension of intellectual differences, its composition made it strongly resistant to the influence of the general social situation. One gets the impression that the great world events that took place from 1959 to 1962 were not adequately reflected within this group. Even John XXIII's most significant actions, such as the issuing of the encyclical *Mater et Magistra*, seem hardly to have impinged upon the atmosphere of the preparations. An example of this can be seen in the drafting of a few documents on the pastoral approach toward communists, who for the majority seemed to be the problem.

What was approaching? Would it be an insignificant meeting of ecclesiastical dignitaries? Or would it be a meeting of global significance and a transition to a new epoch?

2

Toward a Conciliar Consciousness (1962)

The Church Rejoices

Finally, on October 11, 1962, the solemn opening of the Council was celebrated. Several thousand Council fathers, experts, and representatives were packed into the undeniably evocative setting of the Vatican basilica. European bishops, numbering 1,041, made up less than half of the Council fathers. There were 956 North and South American bishops; 379 bishops from Africa; and more than 300 bishops from Asia. The largest group by nationality was Italian, which numbered 379 bishops, but they made up less than one-fifth of the assembly, a much smaller percentage than in preceding councils. John XXIII began the inaugural address with the words "Mother Church rejoices" *(Gaudet Mater Ecclesia).*[1] The use of Latin and the excitement of the moment prevented many from understanding its importance immediately, but it was the most prominent act of John XXIII's pontificate and among the most ambitious and significant acts of the Catholic Church in the modern era.

The pope had worked with great diligence to express in this address the deep convictions that had urged him to convene the Council. He started preparing the speech no later than January 25, 1959, while more immediate preparations date from February 2, 1962, when the pope fixed the opening of Vatican II for October 11 of that year. It is worth emphasizing that John XXIII wrote this text personally. The manuscript pages were carefully revised; they contain corrections, rearrangements, and additions, all in the pope's own handwriting. The same is true of the typewritten copy, which contains more personal modifications in Roncalli's own hand, testifying to an exacting attention to the revision and perfection of the text.

The first part is dedicated to the nature of the Council, to its convocation and preparation, and to Christ, the Church, and history. Having evoked the centrality of the councils in the life of the Church, the pope situates Vatican II "in the context of the deviations, the needs, and the opportunities

Photo reproduced by courtesy of Giuseeppe Alberigo

On October 1, 1962, a few days before the opening of Vatican II, Pope John was presented with a copy of the Bologna Workshop's monumental edition of *Conciliorum Oecumenicorum Decreta* (The Decrees of the Ecumenical Councils). The pope inscribed the following words in his diary: "A good beginning of the month of the Council. Cardinal Lercaro informs me of his 'Documentation Center' in the company of Don Dossetti and his companions, a pledge of excellent work. They offer me their most precious flower, *Conciliorum Oecumenicorum Decreta*. I encourage them and bless them from my heart." From left to right: Giuseppe Alberigo, Perile P. Joannou, Claudio Leonardi, Cardinal Giacomo Lercaro, Pope John XXIII, Giuseppe Dossetti, Paulo Prodi, Domenico Nucci, and Boris Ulianich.

of the modern age." The new Council is called to be "a solemn celebration of the union of Christ with his Church," constituting an opportunity for "a wider and more objective understanding" of the Church's possibilities in terms of human society and its future, but with a friendly and welcoming attitude, not one of condemnation.

John's appeal was that "the Church, illuminated by the light of the Council, may be enlarged with spiritual riches and look undaunted toward the future, through fitting measures of renewal." It was, therefore, necessary to discern the signs of the times, overcoming the "spiritual tendencies that, although they are full of fervor and zeal, are by no means equipped with an abundant sense of discretion and moderation, seeing in the modern era nothing but transgression and disaster, and claiming that our own age has become worse than previous ones." The pope explicitly declares that he "must dissent from these prophets of doom, who are always announcing some ominous event, almost as if the end of the world were upon us." This part of his speech culminates with the expression of his conviction that all of humanity is heading toward a new cycle of history that bears within itself an "unexpected" and "unforeseen"—that is, an entirely transcendent— meaning for salvation.

The second part deals with a few essential matters: the dynamic relationship between the kingdom of God and human society, the opportunity for a reformulation of essential tenets of the faith (the *depositum fidei*), the choice of an attitude of mercy instead of severity, and the commitment to efforts for Christian unity. Not even here does the pope intend to dictate the order of the day for the work of the Council; his contribution to the passage of the Church into a new era of history is, instead, that of accentuating the spirit of the Council. On the basis of tradition, he continues,

> the Christian, Catholic, and apostolic spirit of the entire world is awaiting a leap forward toward an assimilation of doctrine and a formation of consciences in greater fidelity to authentic teaching. But even this must be elaborated and presented according to the forms of inquiry and literary expression proper to modern thought. The substance of the ancient doctrine of the *depositum fidei* is one thing, and the manner of presenting it is another.

This is the salient point of the Council, and it is in relation to this that John XXIII expresses his hope for a "magisterium of a predominantly pastoral nature, [which would move] toward the needs of today, showing the validity of doctrine instead of issuing condemnations."

Finally, Vatican II is situated by the pope within the perspective of the unity of all Christians, indeed, of the entire human race. Pope John XXIII emphasizes a threefold emanation of the mystery of unity: that of Catholics among themselves, that of all Christians, and that of the members of non-Christian religions. What is striking is the absence of any sort of blame accorded to non-Catholics, although the pope did not renounce the task of reaffirming the Catholic Church's fidelity to Christ and to the successors of Peter, as well as his commitment to working for the restoration of the "great mystery of unity." In this sense also—and more so than in any other—the speech showed the well-developed result of reflection and long experience. Since his mission in Bulgaria, which began in 1925, Roncalli's contact with the ecumenical movement had never diminished, and it had fostered such an internalization and mastery of the issue of Christian unity that this became one of the essential and characteristic elements of the "dowry" that he brought to the office of the papacy.

The text concludes with a lengthy quote from *De Unitate* by Cyprian of Carthage, showing Christ as the vital center of the ecclesial dynamic of unity and multiplicity and inviting his listeners to place Vatican II in a perspective of salvation, as an opportunity for the Catholic Church to reexamine itself in order to establish as effective a presence as possible among human beings.

The significance and liberating implications of this speech were slow to be understood. I remember the sense of excitement and shock as our little group from Bologna gathered around Giuseppe Dossetti and listened to the message with lively interest and with trepidation. It seemed to us much more powerful than one would have expected a speech under such circumstances to be. This text demanded great attention and an attentive examination of its meaning.

The Council fathers immediately focused upon the selection of the commissions, the working groups. The selections they made would afford the first opportunity to evaluate the composition of the groups responsible for guiding the assembly. Through the initiative of some of the European cardinals (Cardinal Liénart of France and Cardinal Frings of Germany), a request was made on October 13 for a delay of the elections, which had been scheduled for that day. This would give the Council fathers time to establish contact with one another and to prevent what would otherwise have been inevitable: the confirmation of the preparatory commissions as the Council's working groups.

This initiative created some surprise and excitement because it was the first hint of the conciliar consciousness of the assembly, which, although it was for the most part composed of persons unfamiliar with the mechanisms of such a gathering, would not submit passively to the decisions made by the preparatory bodies. So, on October 16, the commissions were elected on the basis of lists provided by the various bishops' conferences. The result was the predominance of bishops from Central Europe and from the other continents over the "Latin" bishops (from Italy and Spain). Many of the members of the preparatory commissions were not elected.

When the results were made known, it was learned that Pope John had added a clause to the regulations according to which the fathers who had received the highest number of votes were elected to the commissions, not only those who had received an absolute majority of votes; this was an unequivocal demonstration of his respect for the will of the assembly. One-third of the places on the commissions had been reserved for papal appointment; with the pope's selections, the number of Italians on the commissions was significantly increased. The Curia obtained its request that, as for the preparatory commissions, the presidency of each of the Council's commissions would be entrusted to the prefect of the corresponding Roman congregation. The French Dominican theologian M.-D. Chenu was convinced that it was

> necessary that the way be prepared for the Council's decisions through a broad declaration which would proclaim the plan of salvation, in the manner of the gospel and with the prophetic perspective of the Old and New Testaments . . . This declaration would be issued to a humanity whose greatness and misery represent, among errors and failures, a longing for the light of the gospel . . . It would proclaim

the fraternal unity of all people, beyond borders and races and re-
gimes, in their rejection of violent solutions and their love for peace,
a manifestation of the kingdom of God.[2]

On October 20 the Council approved a brief message for the world
dedicated to the Church's presentation of itself and its mission and intended to demonstrate the Catholic Church's solidarity with humanity in
regard to the major problems of the modern world:

> We turn our attention continually toward the anguish that afflicts
> people today, and our concern goes first of all to the most humble,
> the poorest, the weakest. Following Christ's example, we feel com-
> passion for the crowds that suffer from hunger, misery, and igno-
> rance; we turn constantly to those who, deprived of the necessary
> help, have still not attained the kind of life that they deserve. For
> these reasons, as we carry out our work we will keep in serious con-
> sideration everything that is conducive to the dignity of the human
> person, and that contributes to the true fraternity of peoples.[3]

It was a message of interest for humanity, especially in regard to the aspects of peace and social justice. As one African bishop noted, "We were
no longer closed up in our little huts." The conclusion of the message
echoed the quotation from the Acts of the Apostles used by John XXIII in
his opening discourse *Gaudet Mater Ecclesia*: "We possess neither riches
nor earthly power, but we place our trust in the power of the Spirit." The
message did not receive a lot of press coverage and was quickly forgotten,
but it showed the urgency of expressing the Church's concern to those
outside of it, and it described the Church in Council as a meeting of the
"successor of the apostles" who made up a single "apostolic body" of which
the head was the "successor of Peter." The assembly thus emphasized immediately the insufficiency of the preparatory plans, in which these concerns were absent.

John XXIII decided that the first topic the Council would work on would
be the liturgy; this was the aspect of the Church's life in which renewal had
already made the most progress, and the preparatory project for it was the
only one that had found a consensus among the bishops, who had already
been sensitized by the liturgical movement. So, from October 22 to November 13 the assembly discussed liturgical reform; votes taken on both
the entirety of the schema and each individual chapter always showed a
great majority in favor, in spite of the tenacious resistance of a minority
stubbornly opposed to any innovation.

Thus among these people, who had not even known one another before, a convergence of sentiments and viewpoints was gradually manifested,
giving rise to a completely unexpected and spontaneous majority, a very
large number of votes that tended to converge on the major topics of the

Council. It was a gradual but rapid process, without any planning or management; the Council fathers were simply becoming aware of their role and of the vast and unforeseen horizons of the Council itself. Their favorable response did not concern the proposed text on liturgical reform alone; it also expressed the conviction that the time of fear, the era of the Church as a secure fortress, was over. The adoption of the vernacular languages, at least for some parts of the liturgical celebrations, was the most evident innovation, if not the most important. It was a way of reestablishing contact with the common people, of proposing the gospel message in a comprehensible way. The discussion brought forth significant elements of theology that had been overlooked until then; that is, the local Church, or diocese, regained its centrality as an authentic Christian community in which the profession of the faith transcends the level of the individual to become a communitarian act around the altar of the bishop, who reacquired his dimension of authentic successor of the apostles.

Just as significant was the importance accorded to the liturgy of the Word—the first part of the Mass, dedicated to the reading and explanation of texts taken from sacred scripture—compared to that of the liturgy of the Eucharist. After the Council of Trent the latter had monopolized the attention of theologians, so much so that it was the only part of the Mass that the faithful were required to attend in order to fulfill their Sunday and feast day obligation. In spite of intense work and wide consensus, the great number of amendments presented and the pope's desire not to force the pace of the Council's progress made it advisable to delay the closing of this matter until the next phase of the Council. The announcement of the delay, made on November 19, deflated another widespread preconception that the Council would approve all of the preparatory material almost by common acclamation and in a very short time.

Meanwhile, an informal group of Council fathers and periti especially sensitive to the problems of poverty had begun working in earnest at the end of October at the Belgian College in Rome, through the initiative of Paul Gauthier, a worker-priest. The group came to be known as the Church of the Poor Group. Although its members came from various backgrounds and experiences, they recognized that a gap had been created between the Church and the poor—in both the industrialized countries and the Third World—and that the origin of this gap could be found in the identification of the Church with capitalist society. Although this group applied significant pressure to many fathers, it always remained at the margins of the Council. Even the initiative of Paul VI in October 1963 to ask Cardinal Lercaro—an active member of the group—to make concrete proposals for Church life (which were presented a year later) did not come to anything. In early November, Cardinal Lercaro—who was involved in the work of the Liturgical Commission—asked Dossetti to take his place in the group advocating in behalf of the poor. In addition to his participation in Gauthier's group, Dossetti—as Lercaro's "private" theologian—created a compact network of contacts among bishops and theologians. This network produced and spread observations on the preparatory schemata. Through this intervention the "Bologna workshop" followed the Council's work from that time on, and the research that members of the group had done on the history of ecumenical councils just a few years earlier proved particularly helpful. During the Council the refuge of Dossetti and the rest of the Bologna group was the hospitality of Laura and Pia Portoghesi on Via della Chiesa Nuova.

On November 14, 1962, general debate on "The Sources of Revelation" was begun. The work was directed by the Preparatory Theological Commission. This occasion saw an encounter of a number of fairly diverse mentalities, cultural backgrounds, and theological viewpoints. The use of the plural "sources" in the title indicated the accommodation of a distinctly anti-Protestant theological tenet, opposition to the principle of "scripture alone," which Martin Luther and the Protestants had always upheld. But this clear sense of opposition seemed to be offset by further elaboration and the recovery of the importance of the Bible that was taking place, not only in Catholic theology, but also in ecclesial and spiritual experience. By then, the prevalent opinion was that the word of God alone was the primary source of Christian revelation. There were also some delicate pastoral and ecumenical problems connected to this difficulty, which immediately became clear when the schema was criticized radically and in great detail by those who refused to place oral tradition on the same level as the word of God as fixed in the Bible.

On November 20, voting on the admissibility of the schema as the basis for the Council's work revealed a surprise: there were 1,368 votes against, and only 822 in favor. The assembly was not made up of "yes men" ready to accept any sort of proposal. But it seemed that according to the rules a two-thirds majority was necessary, not only to approve a text, but also to reject one. In that case, the work on the two sources of revelation would have to be based on the schema, in spite of the fact that 60 percent of the Council fathers had rejected it.

After hearing appeals from leaders of the majority, John XXIII decided to protect the Council's freedom and, out of respect for the unmistakable will of the assembly, decreed that the two-thirds majority needed for the approval of a text was not required to reject it. So the preparatory document was thrown out and a new one had to be created by a mixed commission (not the Doctrinal Commission monopolized by Cardinal Ottaviani, the head of the Holy Office) composed of the members of both the Theological Commission and the Secretariat for Christian Unity. This was the beginning of a successful tactic, that of assigning tasks involving serious responsibility for many of the crucial aspects of the Council's work to the secretariat and its head, Jesuit Cardinal Augustin Bea. Another pillar of the Curia's hegemony over the Council's work had been demolished. This created concern in the circles close to the Curia, especially among the

Italians. On November 24, fourteen of the cardinals, including Siri, Bacci, Traglia, Ruffini, and Marella, sent the pope a letter expressing their fears about the tendencies that had emerged in the Council during the debate on the sources of revelation. Nothing came of the letter.

On November 23, the Council entered the last phase of the initial period. There was still a great deal of work to be done, but the deadline had been set for December 8. Two other documents were added to the day's business (one on the means of social communication and one on the unity of the Church). And on that same November 23 the most anticipated document of all, the schema on the Church, was also distributed. Many thought that this document needed to balance the definitions of the infallibility and primacy of the pope proclaimed at Vatican Council I.

During the general debate the document on social communications (radio, television, the press, and so on) was criticized for its wordiness, which was seen as inappropriate for a conciliar decree; it also seemed too preoccupied with the reaffirmation of the Church's rights and moralistic concerns. But, more important, this topic simply did not interest the assembly, which wanted to address more relevant questions. So, on November 27, a conciliatory proposal from the Council of Presidents was accepted: the substance of the schema was approved on the condition that the commission would reduce the document to a few essential propositions.

The very fact that a schema on Christian unity had been submitted to the Council was an important new development in view of Catholics' age-old and continual mistrust of ecumenism. Nevertheless, the preparatory text had been developed by the Commission for the Oriental Churches, and so it took into consideration only relations with the Orthodox tradition in the context of *uniatism*, a term indicating the effort to promote Churches that were Eastern in rite but subject to Rome. These were obviously viewed with hostility by the Orthodox Churches. But two different presentations of ecumenical issues had been developed: one by the Secretariat for Christian Unity and another by the Theological Commission. This was a result of poor coordination of the preparatory work. So it was inevitable that the outline of this matter would be delayed until it could be examined jointly by the Doctrinal Commission, the Commission for the Oriental Churches, and the Secretariat for Christian Unity.

During that same period Cardinal Ottaviani proposed discussing a very brief schema about the Virgin Mary. Many of the fathers thought it would be strange to consider this matter apart from discussions about the Church, which seemed the natural context within which Mary would be situated theologically, that is, within the mystery of the people of God. Moreover, discussing Mary within the context of the teaching about the Church would avoid difficulties and misunderstandings with the other Christian traditions, which were often uncomfortable with the excesses of Catholic devotion to Mary. The Council of Presidents was fairly sensitive to these issues and even more so to the fathers' eagerness and impatience to turn to the schema on the Church.

It began to seem that the success of the Council would depend strictly upon the Church's manner of defining itself. This was all the more true in that the liturgical reform had foreshadowed some significant ideas about the Church that corrected the excessively institutional and juridical approach of recent centuries.

First Steps

Because of this increasing focus, the six sessions of the Council beginning December 1 were dedicated to an examination of the project concerning the Church. The document on this subject comprised eleven chapters and eighty pages. This debate was one of the high points displaying how the Council's self-awareness had made gigantic strides during its two months of work; by this time the assembly was capable of expressing deliberately chosen points of view and of recognizing its own authoritative leaders. The resulting schema was considered one of the best of those approved by the Preparatory Theological Commission, and in spite of the fact that it was expounded by the highly authoritative Cardinal Ottaviani, serious objections were raised concerning both the manner of its development and the point of view that inspired it.

The text seemed to have little to do with recent theological contributions and seemed also to be too closely linked to an image of the Church as a society that needed to be governed by juridical norms. In this context, obviously, the institutional aspects of the Church were dominant. The architects of the project missed the importance of the mystery at the heart of the Church, just as they ignored any sense of ecumenism, especially when it came to facing the crucial question of just who the members of the Church are (all the baptized—Orthodox, Anglicans, and Protestants—or only those baptized into Catholicism?). Also, the bishop's office was still being presented as subordinate to the prerogatives of the papacy.

The debate was a precious opportunity for the Council to discuss deep issues and to realize, perhaps for the first time, that its work was not strictly intended for the Catholic Church itself but had much wider implications that were moving toward similarly broad horizons. The Council's opening address had delineated the Church's new situation as an open community with no natural defenses, available to the needs of humanity, a situation that was taking on ever more precise and demanding features. A tightly focused series of interventions on the topic showed, from different but complementary points of view, how the contemporary Christian conscience was substantially different from the spirit of the preparatory schema.

Cardinal Suenens of Belgium, who was very close to John XXIII, explained the demands that had inspired an alternative plan, one that had been formulated by the intellectual circles of the University of Louvain. His concern was that of determining the central theme of all the Council's later work. He was proposing a Council entirely dedicated to the theme of the Church, which would be developed in two stages: the Church within itself, and the Church in relation to others. The first part would explain the Church as the mystery of Christ living within his faithful (the mystical body). Then it would be necessary to explain what a pastoral renewal of the Church would entail: mission, catechesis, sanctification, and prayer. In its dialogue with the world, the Church's commitments would need to include human rights, social justice, the evangelization of the poor, peace, and war.

The mystery of Christ's vital relationship with his Church, through which he imparts salvation to humanity, seemed to Cardinal Montini—the future Paul VI—the central point around which the Council's reconsideration of ecclesiology must revolve. It seemed clear that the great majority of the fathers did not recognize themselves in the triumphalism of the preparatory schema, as Bishop De Smedt of Belgium said openly. This was in spite of the fact that the text had been prepared by the most authoritative exponents of the Congregation of the Holy Office. What was desired was a greater attention to the nature of the Church as the people of God (as expressed by German Cardinal Döpfner) and its mission to humanity (spoken of by Cardinal Suenens).

Archbishop Lercaro of Bologna proposed the idea of the Church of the poor as the guiding theme of the Council's work, presenting it "as an organizing principle, a point of clarification and cohesion for all the topics treated up to now" and all the work still to come. The presence of Christ in the poor—two-thirds of humanity—was joined to the two other profound realities of the mystery of Christ in the Church: the Eucharist and the episcopacy. This perspective, which was perhaps the most original and prophetic of the first phase and was welcomed with particular enthusiasm by the bishops from the Third World, concluded—partly because of administrative considerations—this phase of the work and confirmed its significance.

Even though there had not been any definitive voting, no one could deny the general impression that a new way of understanding the Church had been manifested, that a new ecclesiology was beginning to appear at the Council. The assembly concluded the first phase of its work in a state of uncertainty; none of the schemata taken into consideration had been approved. And apart from the project for liturgical reform, none of the preparatory work had found general agreement. The fact that no decisive vote had been taken might have given the impression that this great assembly was not capable of expressing clear judgments. Was this an indication that John XXIII's intuition could not be made a reality?

The fact was that these first two months had been a sort of warmup period for an episcopacy unaccustomed to exercising real responsibility for the worldwide Church and a bit disoriented by the freedom the pope had granted to the Council. The Italian and Spanish bishops, who were accustomed to complete dependence upon Rome and were doubtful of the other European bishops' fidelity to the pope, remained in isolation for the first few weeks, avoiding both confrontation and contact with the others. The Latin American, African, and Asian bishops felt excluded from the Central European nucleus composed of the French, the Germans, the Austrians, the Belgians, and the Dutch. But the atmosphere of the Council gradually encouraged each participant to contribute his own experience, culture, and competence for the benefit of all, bringing about the conditions for the effective exercise of the episcopal charism. It seemed highly unlikely that Catholicism could emerge so rapidly from the long period of the Counter-Reformation, in which a respectful and often passive fidelity to Rome had prevailed. What would happen to the Council now?

The approach of a pause of nine months in the assembly's work raised lively concerns. The fear was that, after all the bishops returned to their own dioceses, the same atmosphere and outlook that had dominated Rome during the preparation would dominate again. Moreover, the rules made no provisions to obviate this eventuality. At that time the group from Bologna, which, like others, had established useful contacts and relationships in various directions, made proposals intended to guarantee that the work entrusted to the commissions during the assembly's long vacation would proceed according to the guidelines established by John XXIII and shared by so many of the bishops, rather than according to the approach shown during the preparations. Two acts of clarification just before the recess, on December 5 and 6, reassured the Council participants. One of these was the distribution to the fathers of a booklet in which the numerous preparatory schemata were condensed into twenty topics that accepted, at least formally, the areas of concentration that had been suggested by many of the participants. More relevant still was John XXIII's decision to establish criteria in order to ensure that the Council's activity would continue during the upcoming recess.[4] At the same time he created a Coordinating Commission whose very title demonstrated the acceptance of requests for a qualified and authoritative body to manage and organize the Council's work, especially during the assembly's vacation. The main significance of these actions, and also of the letter the pope sent to all the bishops for the Feast of the Epiphany, was to render explicit and definitive the harmony that had been created between the pope and the great majority of the Council. The result was a genuine shift in the atmosphere of the assembly, as would become clear in the first months of 1963.

Perhaps no one noticed at that time the uneven character of the convergences that had been occurring. Indeed, while on an emotional level the majority of the Council appeared united in distancing itself from the preparatory work and in sharing the perspectives expressed by the pope, there were substantial differences within this majority on a theological level. These disagreements would emerge later and frequently diminish the incisiveness of the Council's work. For their part, however, the media and public opinion had clearly discerned the significance of what was happening at St. Peter's. In fact, attention to the progress of the Council had grown well beyond the boundaries of Catholicism. The bishops' lively discussions, the manifestation of deep disagreements, and the pope's discreet participation provoked a wave of general and unexpected attention.

The 1962–1963 Interval between Sessions and a New Phase of Preparation

Although the first period of activity had produced no conclusive decisions, it had produced an imposing quantity of material that the commissions now needed to sort through and evaluate. John XXIII had appointed the Cardinals Confalonieri, Döpfner, Liénart, Spellman, Suenens, and Urbani (two Italians, three Central Europeans, and one North American) to the Coordinating Commission. Cardinal Secretary of State Cicognani was made president of this group. The commission provided a fundamental orientation for the work of evaluating the material produced during the first phase of the Council, beginning with the session that met from January 21 to January 27, when the schemata were drastically reduced to seventeen. Upon his ascension to the papacy following John XXIII's death on June 3, 1963, Paul VI added three more members (Agagianian, Lercaro, and Roberti), and four more sessions were held before the reopening of the Council.[5] Thus Vatican II was freed from its bondage to the preparatory work, although many of the elements and formulations produced during that phase were reintroduced into the texts later submitted to the Council. Continuity and novelty were balanced with results that were not always convincing.

In closing the first phase of the Council, Pope John XXIII had carefully asserted that the solemn session on December 8 did not at all imply "a halt in the work; on the contrary, what is waiting for all of us will be extremely relevant, unlike the pauses in other councils . . . The Council itself will remain very much open during the next nine months of recess for the ecumenical sessions properly so called." This message was repeated in the Epiphany letter to all the bishops referred to earlier. John emphasized that "the Council receives its directives from the pope, who convened it, but at the same time it is the bishops' task to safeguard its free development . . . The Council fathers are responsible for proposing, discussing, and preparing the sacred deliberations in the appropriate form." Such indications were particularly significant given that it was certain by that time that Pope John, who was incurably ill, would not be able to participate in the resumption of the Council. They helped dispel the impression that the suspension of the work, together with the pope's illness, would delay the reopening of the Council or postpone it indefinitely, even though the work was scheduled to begin again in the middle of September 1963. Under the impulse of the Coordinating Commission, the conciliar commissions pursued their work rapidly; their work was frequently elaborated by subcommissions entrusted with the task of discussing the individual topics in greater detail. Once the commissions had elaborated them in accordance with the indications that had emerged during the first period, the projects were passed along for the scrutiny of the Coordinating Commission before being submitted for the pope's approval and distributed to the fathers.

It was clear by now that the organizing theme of Vatican II was the Church. Dissatisfaction with the text presented by the preparatory theological commission led to the circulation of many alternative projects among the fathers. The most active theological schools struggled with one another over the conception of the Church. In addition to the project of the Roman School, there was a Belgian project that had been developed by theologians (one French, one German) from the ancient Catholic University of Louvain. Their project was characterized by an intense biblical inspiration and was supported by a group of bishops, including one from Chile, who revealed the vigor and tenacity of the Latin American Church.[6] The circles that would later be referred to as the minority made an effort to reject these alternative projects, maintaining that these would not receive the pope's approval, unlike the ones produced by the preparatory commissions. But it was quickly clarified that John XXIII had not approved the preparatory work but merely had authorized its being sent to the bishops. There was a big difference between the two.

During the last ten days of February 1963 the Theological Commission formed a working group for the document *De Ecclesia* with the recommendation that it proceed not with the creation of a new schema but with the elaboration of the preparatory one. It was a desperate attempt to save the foundation of all the preconciliar work. But the group, in keeping with the outlook that had emerged from the discussions during the previous December, decided to take as its starting point the preparatory outline produced by Belgian theologian Gérard Philips, which began with the words "Light of the Nations" *(Lumen Gentium).* So it began to create a new document, after all. The various phases of this work kept the subcommission busy until June 1963.

Instead of the twelve chapters of the preparatory schema, the new one contained only four: the mystery of the Church, its hierarchical makeup, the laity and the people of God, and the religious life. While this led to a profound renewal of the document's structure, Msgr. Philips had used more than a few passages from the preparatory text in order to reduce the opposition to the new document from the "Roman" theologians. The result was something of a hodge-podge.

The first chapter was dedicated to the Church as the mystery of salvation, relegating the juridical dimension to a secondary role. The social philosophy of the Church as a perfect society was definitively abandoned. The second chapter confronted the crucial theme of the relationship between the pope and the bishops, attempting to break through the isolation of the papal office that had developed particularly after the conflicts of the Reformation and the definitions of Vatican Council I, which had exaggerated the personal dimension of the papacy. It was not a matter of resolving the juridical problem of precisely establishing the balance of power and the respective spheres of influence for the bishops and the pope. Rather, it was necessary to recover the essential sacramental meaning of the bishop's ministry and the historical sense of the succession of the apostolic college. Beyond the distortions involved in defining the Catholic Church as a monarchy, the relationship between the pope and the bishops could recover its great depth of fraternity, communion, and reciprocal support. The third chapter underwent the most extensive revision, because it took ongoing discussion to clarify the fundamental concept of the people of God, which established the fundamental equality of all Christians by virtue of their baptism. Moreover, the category "people of God," an important one in the Old Testament, restored the sense of the Church as a pilgrim on the path of history. The fourth chapter, finally, was in reality dedicated to all Christians' vocation to holiness, rather than to the "religious" vocation as lived out in the various orders.

At the same time the other commissions were proceeding fairly rapidly with revisions of their projects. The one on the liturgy was ready by the second half of May, overcoming attempts by members of the Curia to block it, which had paralyzed the commission's work for a long time. At the beginning of March the reformulation of the schema on revelation was also finished. The relationship between scripture and tradition was not resolved, but it wasn't compromised, either. The formula of the "two sources" was abandoned and the fact that Christian revelation is a unity with a single origin was reaffirmed, but it was left to later exegetical and theological elaborations to clarify the relationship between the Bible and tradition. The project was dedicated above all to the centrality of the word of God in the entire life of Christians and the Church.

The Secretariat for Christian Unity produced a text on the Catholic Church's commitment to ecumenism, situating it in a completely fresh perspective in comparison with the preceding centuries. The project it produced began from the developments in the ecumenical movement and sought to translate into practical terms the vision of a Church open to dialogue with its "separated brethren." The first chapter was dedicated to the "mystery of unity," abandoning the usual Catholic accusations of the responsibility of the heretics and schismatics and acknowledging instead the "mystery of division," the existence of shared responsibility and other factors. The second considered the practice of ecumenism, and the third was dedicated to relations with separated Christians: the "Oriental Churches," on the one hand, and on the other, the "communities born in the sixteenth century," meaning the Protestants and Anglicans. The fourth chapter treated the Church's attitude toward non-Christian religions, especially Judaism, and the fifth was dedicated to religious liberty. So two delicate topics, anti-Semitism and freedom of conscience, entered the rolls of the Council's business.

Various other issues (on bishops, missions, and so on) were restructured by their respective commissions. A mixed commission was created to produce the seventeenth and final schema, on the relationship between the Church and the world. Under the supervision of Cardinal Suenens, the commission sought to revise a number of the preparatory projects and, above all, to respond to the increasingly insistent requests that the condition of the Church within history be characterized by friendship with humanity instead of the old hostility.

From John XXIII to Paul VI: Would the Council Die or Continue?

Pope John XXIII's health steadily declined during the first months of 1963, but this did not prevent him from following closely the work being carried out between sessions or from publishing the encyclical *Pacem in Terris*. In the encyclical he broke free from the centuries-old theological tradition on war, denying that there could be any such thing as a just war in the atomic age. For the first time he addressed not only the members of the Church but all people of good will and asked Catholics to collaborate with them all. The death of the pope on Pentecost Sunday, June 3, 1963, constituted a spiritual event that drew the attention of much of the world. He had inaugurated a new era for the Church and revived the essential themes of charity and unity emphasizing the strict connection between renewal of spirituality and renewal of the structures of the Church, along with the reformulation of doctrine.

In addition to the sadness felt at the death of a man who had lived profoundly his role as father and teacher, some anxiety emerged over whether or not the Council would continue. Would it die with him? What would his successor do? There was no hiding the fact that the Council had many powerful opponents, especially in Roman circles, and no one could force the new pope to continue it if he didn't want to. The brief conclave held June 19–21, 1963, elected the Archbishop of Milan, Cardinal Giovanni Battista Montini, who took the name Paul VI. Cardinal Montini had been a member of the Central Preparatory Commission for the Council and had contributed to the first period of work. More than anything else, while commemorating the newly deceased pope in Milan, he explicitly committed himself to continuing his legacy, asking, "Could we really abandon a path that has been so masterfully marked out by John XXIII, even into the future? There is reason to believe that we couldn't."

The confirmation of this outlook came with Paul VI's first message, when he said, "The most substantial portion of this pontificate will be occupied by the continuation of the ecumenical Council Vatican II, toward which the eyes of all people of good will are turned." Despite those words, problems were not lacking, and a pamphlet entitled *La difficile scelta* (The Difficult Choice), published in 1964 in Italian by Michael Serafian, reflected this situation and provoked heated discussions. On June 27, 1963, it was announced not only that the pope had arranged for the continuation of the Council, but also that he had fixed September 29 as the starting date. Only two weeks had gone by, the same length of time as the see of Peter had been vacant.

In a letter sent from Weisskirchen/Saar on August 11, 1963, Hubert Jedin told me that he shared Serafian's perplexity about Paul VI. He was convinced of the new pontiff's willingness to continue the Council, but he also knew that the differences between John XXIII and Paul VI in terms of education, personality, and experience were many and deep and that their outlooks must necessarily be different. The next day I responded that more time was needed to understand the new pope's point of view. I hoped that the next session would at least resolve the problem of the Council's direction with the appointment of a small college of legates.

The experience of the Council's first period suggested to Pope Paul that he address immediately the question of making organizational changes that would guarantee the greatest possible efficiency for the assembly. The most unsatisfying aspect was the management of the work; the presiding body was too large and varied to take care of this with the necessary timeliness and authoritativeness. Some were hoping that the pope would appoint a legate, a papal representative who would preside over the Council's work. During the summer of 1963 the group from Bologna had prepared a detailed plan for modifications that, after a complicated roundabout of contacts and personal influence, came to form the basis of the pope's decisions.

In the end, Paul VI favored the creation of a small college of *moderators*, who would be the liaisons between the pope and the assembly, each of the moderators taking a turn at directing the assembly's work. Just before the Council was reconvened, Cardinals Agagianian, Döpfner, Lercaro, and Suenens were designated to assume this responsibility. Cardinal Agagianian, who was of Armenian origin, was a supporter of the Roman Curia and the Council's minority group; the others were the bishops of three important European episcopal sees (Munich, Bologna, and Malines-Brussels) and authoritative representatives of the majority.

Paul VI also decided to create the category of *auditors* at the Council, which would permit allowing a number of lay people, who had been completely excluded before, to participate. Finally, before the resumption of the work, the pope thought it opportune to make a public statement reassuring the Roman Curia that it alone, and not the Council, was responsible for reforming itself. By granting the Curia the right to make its own reforms, the pope lessened its resistance to the Council, although this came at the price of causing disappointment and bad feeling in the assembly. Paul VI would provide for the reform of the Roman Curia with the document *Regimini Ecclesiae* on August 15, 1967. Before the opening of the Council's second phase, the pope decided to create the Secretariat for Non-Christians, which was in a way analogous to the Secretariat for Christian Unity.

Shadows and Light in the First Experience

There were very few who consciously related the Council to the changed conditions of the world, which was still recovering from an immense and brutal conflict (World War II, 1939–45), and which was still divided by opposing ideologies and overshadowed by the threat of nuclear conflict. The scenario of a humanity that wanted peace but could not obtain it was far from the minds of the Council fathers, as was the image of a world caught up in an exciting period of scientific, economic, and technological development but afflicted by serious social inequalities. Traditionally, the councils were intended to evaluate already existing situations of *ecclesiastical* conflict, motivated by unsolved problems that had arisen in the past. But the context of Vatican II was beginning to be different.

The transition from the long preparations for the Council to its actual unfolding found almost everyone unprepared. Many believed that the Council would be brief and would consist of the approval of the many documents painstakingly composed by the preparatory commissions and then presented by the Central Preparatory Commission. The majority of the bishops streaming in to Rome for the first session had a weak knowledge of past councils. They preferred to ask, "What does the pope want?" in regard to both the Council's decisions and its duration. The difficulty of attaining a *global* vision of the Church's situation in the midst of world history had still not been overcome, even though the hopes created by the announcement of the Council had been shared by many of the bishops.

As we have seen, the beginning of the Council's work was characterized by an atmosphere of subservient devotion on the part of the majority of the bishops toward the Roman Curia and toward the preparatory work that the Curia had dominated. Given such attitudes, it was easy to believe that the pope's authorization to send the schemata to the bishops constituted his approval of their contents. Enthusiasm, disorientation, a commitment to inquiry, boredom, and disappointment came and went by turns during the weeks between October 11 and December 8, 1962. The idyllic image of the Council collapsed as a complicated procedure defined the assembly's identity. The bishops' lack of experience with working in groups, not to mention in a grand assembly, necessitated an accelerated and laborious training period. Cardinal Gracias, from India, expressed this fittingly at the beginning of December when he said that "we have learned to walk with our own legs."

The discussion on the liturgy had facilitated a beginning to the Council that was very concrete and not too demanding; the debate had begun, but there were no harsh tensions yet. Many of the participants were comfortable with this familiar set of topics, and this had helped them to overcome their initial timidity. Some of them, perhaps, had not fully realized the doctrinal implications of some of the crucial passages in the document, *Sacrosanctum Concilium*, as, for example, when the Council affirmed that

> the liturgy is the summit toward which the activity of the Church is directed; it is also the fount from which all her power flows. For the goal of the apostolic endeavor is that all who are made sons of God by faith and baptism should come together to praise God in the midst of his Church, to take part in the Sacrifice and to eat the Lord's Supper.
>
> The liturgy, in its turn, moves the faithful filled with "the paschal sacraments" to be "one in holiness"; it prays that "they hold fast in their lives to what they have grasped by their faith." The renewal in the Eucharist of the covenant between the Lord and man draws the faithful and sets them aflame with Christ's insistent love. From the liturgy, therefore, and especially from the Eucharist, grace is poured forth upon us as from a fountain, and the sanctification of men in Christ and the glorification of God to which all other activities of the Church are directed. (*SC*, 10)[7]

Moreover, in regard to the presence of Christians at the liturgy, the final text affirmed that

> Mother Church earnestly desires that all the faithful should be led to that full, conscious, and active participation in liturgical celebrations which is demanded by the very nature of the liturgy, and to which the Christian people, "a chosen race, a royal priesthood, a holy nation, a redeemed people" (1 Pet. 2:9, 4–5) have a right and obligation by reason of their baptism. (*SC*, 14)

The centrality of the local Church was also formally confirmed:

> The bishop is to be considered as the High Priest of his flock from whom the life in Christ in his faithful is in some way derived and upon whom it in some way depends. Therefore all should hold in the greatest esteem the liturgical life of the diocese centered around the bishop, especially in his cathedral Church. They must be convinced that the principal manifestation of the Church consists in the full, active participation of all God's holy people in the same liturgical

celebrations, especially in the same Eucharist, in one prayer, at one altar, at which the bishop presides, surrounded by his college of priests and by his ministers. (*SC*, 41)

Attention was drawn again to the importance of the bishops' conferences and the equal standing accorded to the liturgy of the Word and the liturgy of the Eucharist. As would be seen later, these advances were part of a dynamic perspective on the overall conception of the Church and were to affect all later work at the Council.

In less than three days the assembly freed itself from the constraint of the working document on the means of social communications, seeing this as a waste of time. But everyone was eager to discuss the document on the Church, *De Ecclesia*. With the benefit of four decades of hindsight, we can ask ourselves whether—because of the inadequacy of the preparatory schema—the Council was shortsighted in its failure to anticipate the enormous expansion of the spiritual and cultural importance of the media. Was putting aside discussion on this topic a wasted opportunity?

One gets the impression that the Council found itself investigating new problems, or at least gaining new perspectives on familiar problems. During the years 1962 and 1963 a number of issues seemed compelling, and yet achieving them seemed difficult, and perhaps even illusory. The Church needed to move beyond the medieval understanding of the human person. The action of the Holy Spirit had to be restored to the conception of the Church. The eighteenth-century problem of the relationship between Church and state remained to be overcome. And it was necessary to transcend the myopic promotion of Christian unity from the perspective of Catholic conformism and unrealistic hopes for the "return" of separated communities. Those persons were utterly mistaken who thought of as hardly significant, and almost a bit rhetorical, John XXIII's statement that the Councils should complete a "leap forward toward an assimilation of doctrine . . . in greater fidelity to authentic teaching. But even this should be studied and taught according to the forms of inquiry and literary expression proper to modern thought."

The effect of the participation of the many observers from other Christian traditions was felt from the first. Many of them entered discreetly (but much more quickly than many of the bishops) into the dynamics of the assembly. This helps us to understand the growing importance that ecumenical awareness had in the Council's work, beginning with the liturgical constitution itself. In any case, during these months in 1962 the Council assembly increasingly took notice of and assimilated the perspective that the pope had revealed during his speech at the opening of the Council: the urgency of renewing the Church by putting the pastoral approach first.

During the period of adjournment an intense exchange took place between Rome and Constantinople in an effort to bring some observers from Constantinople to the Council or to bypass the problem by establishing a relationship in other forms. Patriarch Athenagoras preferred the idea of establishing a direct theological dialogue between Roman Catholics and the Orthodox in communion with Constantinople. In his view this would take the place of sending observers to Vatican II.[8] Nor was Rome losing sight of the Moscow axis. In July an official Vatican delegation participated in the celebrations for Patriarch Alexei's anniversary of episcopal ordination.

But the Council was not just a little world unto itself; it was a center of contemporary life, beginning with Rome, which was invaded by thousands from all over the globe. There were all sorts of layered and interwoven forms of contact. They ranged from the correspondence that many official delegates carried out with the faithful at home, to the pastoral letters sent at intervals to their dioceses, to the heaps of written and oral information that bombarded the members of the Council, to the media, which were anxious to diffuse information and sometimes unexpectedly influenced events at the Council.

At the resumption of the Council in the fall of 1963, coverage of the Council for the Bologna newspaper *L'Avvenire d'Italia* was provided by the paper's director, Raniero La Valle. His ability to provide clear daily commentaries on the atmosphere of the Council soon had many of the bishops, including non-Italians, reading his paper. In it they found a persuasive synthesis of the assembly's work. During those same weeks a Dutch newspaper editor, Paul Brand, established contact with Karl Rahner, Edward Schillebeeckx, and other theologians with the intention of creating an international theological journal, which would take the name *Concilium*.

Like the Council fathers, the pope also changed as a result of his contact with the assembly. His physical absence from the Council hall expressed his concern not to influence the debates, but it was not meant to indicate lack of interest. The norms to regulate the interval between sessions, his December 8 speech concluding the first phase, and especially the letter to the bishops on Epiphany of 1963 mark stages in a journey of deepening awareness.

A period of adjustment was also needed in terms of the practical daily details. The young clerics of the Roman colleges provided valuable help by accompanying the bishops to their seats. The internal coffee and snack bars became places of rest from the boredom of hearing arguments repeated over and over and the fatigue of listening to a Latin spoken with as many varieties of pronunciation as there were bishops (only the observers enjoyed the privilege of access to translations). But they also provided opportunities for establishing contacts and conducting informal discussions. And, as time went by, the financial aspects of running the Council became worrisome.

After the wearying experience of the election of the commissions, the mechanics of voting were gradually simplified, to such an extent that the process became a model, given the complex composition of the assembly.

The General Secretariat oversaw everything and frequently appropriated the faculty of making decisions. The director of the secretariat, Pericle Felici, became a sort of personification of the Council.

It took just a few weeks for the Council assembly to identify its leading cast, including Bea, Ottaviani, Ruffini, Frings, Léger, Suenens, Lercaro, and, though he was somewhat in the background, Montini. But Larrain of Chile, the Brazilian Hélder Câmara, and Africa's Malula also emerged early on. No less important were the periti, like Tromp, Schillebeeckx, Congar, Ratzinger, Rahner, and Danielou, and the organizers, like the Jesuit Greco, who unified the African bishops, and the rector of the Belgian college in Rome, Prignon, the tireless shadow of Cardinal Suenens.

With the suspension of the work the bishops and periti willingly returned home. Everyone had changed, or was in the process of changing. The momentum that had begun during those first weeks of the Council continued to build, even outside of Rome, in close exchanges of information and points of view among bishops, and especially among theologians, and in many meetings of entire bishops' colleges. The conciliar spirit overflowed within Catholicism and fostered new expectations even on the part of general public opinion. The pope's intervention in the Cuban crisis, the encyclical *Pacem in Terris*, and the death of John XXIII received unprecedented attention. In some instances the anticipation of liturgical renewal permitted a more vivid sense of the arrival of a new season.

John XXIII's invitation to keep interest in the Council alive, found in his letter for Epiphany of 1963, had not fallen on deaf ears. In fact, even where the bishops had not yet organized themselves into conferences, the topics of the Council were discussed and elaborated upon in collegial meetings, as well as in written correspondence. The creative ferment prompted by the Council gave rise to a liberty previously unknown to Catholicism and was a pleasant surprise especially for the observers, who had previously had a fixed image of a sclerotic Roman Church. Apart from and beyond the topics being discussed, a drastic and seemingly unlimited reshuffling of the "certainties" that had even been the foundation of the preparations for Vatican II itself emerged.

The change of pontificate, traditionally a cause of great discontinuity, did not reverse the atmosphere of the Council. Instead, it was the Council that clearly influenced the conclave. But the differences between Pope John and Pope Paul were considerable and did not take long to show themselves, even in relation to the manner of conducting the Council. Above all, a new atmosphere would soon be seen, one determined not only by the character of the new pope but also by his training, his long experience in the service of the Roman Curia, and his deep concern for guaranteeing the greatest possible consensus on the decisions that the Council was preparing to make.

The "Council effect" asserted itself with an overwhelming, unexpected, and contagious energy. Problems that had been dismissed during previous decades (from priestly celibacy to relations with other Christians, from the passivity of the ordinary faithful to the distrust of socialist ideologies) came back to attention, sometimes with a vengeance. Longstanding ecclesial mechanisms of balance and control suddenly seemed inadequate, the ancient authority of the Curia appeared to have been misappropriated, and ordinary methods like centralization and condemnations seemed outdated and foreign to the general conscience. The Holy Office and the Congregation for the Propagation of the Faith, in particular, would pay the price for this. Long-hidden hopes and expectations burst forth into the light of day, and repressed demands found room for expression that previously had been unimaginable. The primacy of repetition, conservation, and passive obedience gradually gave way to inquiry, creativity, and personal responsibility.

The great transformations taking place on the world scene were just as important. These included the end of colonial domination and the accelerated independence of many parts of Africa, the decline of Nikita Khrushchev's power in the Soviet Union, and the tragic assassination of John F. Kennedy in the United States.

3

The Council Matures
(1963)

Growing Pains

Inaugurating the second period of the Council's work on September 29, 1963, Paul VI indicated four objectives: the expression of the Church's theology, its interior renewal, the promotion of Christian unity, and dialogue with the contemporary world. The center of gravity for the work done in 1963 would be the document on the Church. The entire month of October was dedicated to an examination of the new draft of the document, *De Ecclesia*, which had been reworked by Belgian theologian Gérard Philips and presented to the Council on September 30 by Cardinal Ottaviani, the president of the Theological Commission. On October 1 a vote of 2,231 in favor and 43 against approved the text as the basis for discussion.

Discussions began on each of the four chapters of the draft document: on the mystery of the Church in the economy of salvation, from its conception by God the Father to its earthly pilgrimage; on the hierarchical constitution of the Church and on the bishops, called by their consecration to govern the Church in communion (collegiality) among themselves; on the people of God and the laity, founded on the recognition of the participation of all the baptized in the Church's mission; and on the call to holiness as common summons to all believers.

There were three crucial points. One was baptism as the only requirement for belonging to the Church, which had immediate implications for the ecclesial condition of non-Catholic Christians and relations with the other Churches. Another was the greater importance granted to the common priesthood of all believers within a Church seen as the people of God. The third was the difficulty of finding a satisfactory characterization of the call to holiness for all Christians. But the question of episcopal collegiality received special attention from everyone and prompted some bitter opposition. The issue was whether the bishops constituted a single body, a "college," a fraternal union of persons dedicated to a common task, just as the apostles had been "the Twelve."

From October 4 to 16, almost 130 Council fathers addressed the assembly; many of them stressed the close connection between the "college" of the apostles and that of their successors, the bishops, and the fact that episcopal consecration is a true sacrament. Through this sacrament the new bishop becomes part of the body of bishops, the episcopal college, with the purpose and authority not only of administrating the sacraments but also of teaching and governing the Church. He exercises this power within his own local Church, but, in communion with the other bishops and the pope, he also exercises it in regard to the universal Church.

On October 11 an address from Luigi Bettazzi, Auxiliary Bishop of Bologna and one of the youngest of the Council fathers, brought to light— on the basis of historical documentation gathered by the Bologna workshop—the relationship between the bishops and the universal Church in the Roman tradition. His remarks were received with great interest and lively applause:

> The speech was ready on the evening of Wednesday, October 9, but Cardinal Lercaro was in poor spirits following the dissatisfying outcome of the schema on the liturgy. When it comes to anything involving the liturgy, the cardinal is always like a mother in a fit of anxiety before her child, ending up completely disoriented. In any case, he didn't want to deliver the address. So Dossetti asked Bettazzi to come to Chiesa Nuova, and on the afternoon of Thursday, October 11, Bettazzi agreed to speak the next day. Friday morning, Lercaro being the moderator, the youngest bishop of the Council spoke for exactly nine minutes. "Junior et italicus" (The youngest, and an Italian), he said, "I speak in favor of collegiality." And without a doubt he won the Council over, because although at the beginning the fathers were already putting away their notes for the address, little by little a hush spread through the assembly. And at the end there was applause, the first applause there had been so far at that session. This morning [Saturday, October 12], *L'Avvenire d'Italia* ran a headline that was even a bit too enthusiastic ["Open Applause at the Council for the Youngest Italian Bishop"].[1]

The atmosphere at the group from Bologna was expressed well in a letter sent to Dossetti on October 15, which stated:

> Each day we await news of what the Council is bringing to us. From today's newspaper it seems that the Holy Spirit was well rested after Sunday, and was hard at work on Monday. We think of you often and in all things. We are perhaps closer to you than ever before; joined with you in this work we find again the meaning and the explanation

of our encounter long ago on the outskirts of Milan, and we give the Lord heartfelt thanks for this every day, asking him to keep us closely united in this endeavor, and to make us grow a little in his grace.[2]

But others displayed concern that emphasizing the episcopal college would weaken papal authority. This was partly because, in their view, the bishops received the power to govern through papal appointment, as Pius XII had asserted on occasion, and not through their episcopal consecration. Both sides appealed to tradition for support and did not hold back from accusing each other of infidelity to authentic doctrine. This disagreement exposed a widespread conviction that the Church should be organized as a monarchy, with a single head, the pope. But on the other side there was a growing conviction that the monarchical model was out of date and that the current understanding of the faith required a more communitarian organization, as there had been during the first centuries of Christianity. Our group from Bologna dedicated itself especially to documenting how even the most fervent supporters of the papacy had for centuries been convinced that the bishops share with the pope in responsibility for the universal Church.

Another point in chapter three of the schema on the Church also sustained lively opposition, although to a lesser extent. The bishops of Churches suffering from a lack of clergy (for example, in Latin America) asked that the diaconate be restored to the position it had had during the first centuries, a permanent state of service for the Church rather than simply a step toward the priesthood. Many also believed that married men should also be ordained to the diaconate. They were opposed by those who, without taking into account the growing crisis in the post-Tridentine priesthood, were afraid of any relaxation of the discipline of clerical celibacy.

Beginning on October 4, the Council turned to the topic that the pope himself had considered paramount: the relationship between the pope and the bishops. This led in the first place to a universal affirmation of the indisputable value of papal primacy. It remained to be settled how this relationship should be expressed, since the Church was guided by an apostolic college that could not remain a college if it were separated from Peter, its head, just as Peter could not disregard his relationship with the apostolic college.

Catholic News Service

On September 29, 1963, Pope Paul VI opened the second session of the Council.

Moreover, the recognition that episcopal consecration is a true sacrament brought back to the forefront the problem of what the source of the bishop's power is. This could only come directly from God in the very act of consecration. According to this theory the pope's contribution in making bishops concerned only the decision of which diocese the bishop would lead.

This brief summary of topics gives an idea of the seriousness of the Council's task and the level of tension it experienced. Close consideration was given above all to the discussions and problems that had emerged after the definitions of the Vatican Council in 1870, when Prussia's Chancellor Bismarck had maintained that it made no sense to deal with the bishops, since all Church authority had been concentrated in the pope. The very importance of the topics under consideration brought to light some deficiencies in the working procedures. Above all, various people called attention to the impossibility of carrying on a true discussion in the hall. The rules of order required that one sign up in advance to speak and deliver a written summary of the remarks, which would preclude a healthy and immediate exchange of opinion. The response to an address could never come within the same session; there was inevitably a few days' delay. This made the debate less clear, dragging it out and frequently preventing the fathers from really grasping the differences or points of agreement among the various theses that were presented, as would have been possible with an immediate exchange.

Just as serious was the impossibility of knowing how much agreement an individual presentation received in the Council assembly. In a normal parliament, given the presence of organized political groups, an address from any speaker is immediately recognized as having a certain weight and as representing a smaller or larger portion of the assembly. It was much different at the Council. When five fathers argued in favor of the sacramental nature of episcopal consecration, and five argued against it, it was impossible to say if either group had the agreement of a hundred, a thousand, or two thousand fathers—or none of them. These difficulties can be seen in the notes and comments made during those days.

"Will we succeed in saving the Council?" Dossetti asked himself on the evening of Saturday, October 19, amid the red furnishings of the drawing room of Chiesa Nuova, where Einaudi had become president of the Italian republic and La Pira had disseminated his prophesies. The danger is great: "The Council is like a babbling fool that cannot form coherent words and sentences. The danger is that the Curial party will take advantage of this, give the excuse that some sort of conclusion must be reached, and bring a vote on something rather unsubstantial." The Jewish midwives are nowhere to be found, and the commissions are certainly not fostering a spirit of independent inquiry—far from it; as much as possible they are ignoring the real novelties that the Council is proposing. For example, the theological subcommission for collegiality, which seems to think it is going to take care of everything, is headed by Gagnebet, and we can well imagine how pleased he will be to manipulate the schema that has ostentatiously replaced his own. Today Dossetti was expecting to see Medina, whose point of view is unclear. And then there's Philips, who is neither a lion or an eagle.

Another serious matter is the voting procedure: only a *placet* or *non placet* vote may be applied to the amendments; the *placet iuxta modum* may be used only for entire chapters of the schema. So what happens is that after each amendment has been voted on individually, when it comes time to vote on the chapter as a whole this is rejected because of a large number of *placet iuxta modum* votes, which cannot be expressed in any other way. And then these *placet iuxta modum* votes must be interpreted. For example, it can be argued that those who rejected the second chapter of the schema on the liturgy appeared to be innovators insofar as they were asking that the local bishop decide the rules for concelebration, even for the exempt religious orders.[3]

So it was difficult to understand and evaluate the real points of view at the Council assembly. In this situation the commissions ended up with unusual discretionary power, because they were reconsidering all of the amendments proposed by the Council fathers. As a result, for example, a text might be modified according to the will of a small group or some isolated reviewer and not according to the will of the majority. So it was evident that in order to proceed with a valid elaboration of the documents, the commissions needed to understand at least the broad schemata of the majority point of view at the Council.

In light of his previous experience in parliament, Dossetti thought of the possibility of submitting a series of questions for the Council assembly to vote on. The responses to this would show how the Council was broken down into groups. On October 13 he met with us in Bologna to discuss the initiative and a draft of the questions, and in the following days he submitted the questions to the moderators. During the October 15 session the presiding moderator, Cardinal Suenens, announced in the name of his colleagues that some questions on the most controversial doctrinal points would be posed to the fathers. The vote, whether favorable or not, would not be definitive, but it would provide a sense of direction for the commission.

The proposal met with stubborn resistance from the minority, which was hostile to having the meagerness of its presence revealed; it opposed the measure by applying intense pressure on the pope. It was October 23 before the Council of Presidents arrived at a decision to approve the vote, and on October 29 the fathers received a form with the questions, which had been approved by Paul VI. On October 30 the Council voted.

Fifteen days had passed since the first announcement. What had happened during the second half of October? A number of delicate problems had come into relief. There was a confrontation between two theologies of the Church and the episcopate, and there was also a great deal of dissatisfaction with the nomination of the moderators and the trust that Paul VI had placed in them. Some distress had been created by the introduction of the moderators, and even more by the selection of prelates named to this delicate task, three of whom were among the leading exponents of the Council majority. An axis of resistance to their authority was found in the General Secretariat, especially Archbishop Felici, who was seconded by Secretary of State Cardinal Cicognani. Felici was afraid of a reduction of his own sphere of action, especially in the case that the college of moderators would create a permanent secretary of its own, a position that had been filled during the first weeks by Fr. Giuseppe Dossetti.

Felici openly charged Dossetti with depriving him of power and practically taking the direction of the Council away from him. As had always been his style, Dossetti spontaneously stepped aside. By October 14 he was no longer participating in the moderators' meetings. He remained Lercaro's trusted adviser, and, as a peritus, he was very active in formulating proposals for the debates under way, finding a wide audience among other periti and the Council fathers themselves.

To some, raising the level of tension within the Council seemed one way of inducing the new pope to take an attitude different from the partiality that John XXIII had always shown toward the renewal promoted by the Council majority. But it is also true that the delay in voting caused by the opposition fostered greater attention toward problems and questions than might otherwise have been the case. In the end, five questions were submitted to the bishops: (1) whether episcopal consecration is the highest degree of holy orders; (2) whether each consecrated bishop, in communion with the pope and the other bishops, becomes by virtue of his consecration a member of the episcopal college; (3) whether the college of bishops succeeds to the college of the apostles in the task of teaching, sanctifying, and ruling, and whether it possesses—together with its head, the pope, and never without him—full and supreme authority in the Church; (4) whether the bishops enjoy this power by divine right; and (5) whether it would be opportune to restore the diaconate as a distinct and stable degree of the sacred ministry.

The vote brought results that were better than even the most optimistic expectations; in fact, the questions obtained an affirmative response with a majority that varied from 2,123 for the first question to 1,588 for the last. The votes in opposition were never more than 525, on the restoration of the permanent diaconate, and only 34 on the dogmatic question about the sacramental nature of the episcopate. The following November 3, I commented upon the impact of the voting in an article for *L'Avvenire d'Italia*, emphasizing the important shift that had taken place at the Council. With that vote, teaching on the episcopacy was definitively established, and the results could be included in the document *De Ecclesia*. The Council majority assumed leadership for the work with the full, decisive, and explicit agreement of the pope, while the minority would attempt to overcome its own weakness by drawing upon more favorable forces within the Theological Commission.

With the survey of the relative strength of groups in the assembly having been accomplished, the month of October concluded with an exceptional affirmation of the Council's desire for a profound renewal of ecclesial consciousness. The schema on the Church was sent back to the commission with two important changes in the internal order of the topics. The third chapter, which dealt with the people of God, became chapter two. Speaking of the members of the Church as a people whose substantial unity and equality are rooted in baptism created a more direct and natural transition from chapter one, on the mystery of the Church, to the chapter on its members.

Chapter three would now deal with the ecclesiastical hierarchy, its functions, and its ministers. The very succession of topics would demonstrate their decreasing theological importance. On October 29 the assembly had decided, by a small majority, that the schema on the Virgin Mary should be included as the concluding chapter of *De Ecclesia*, situating Mary as an icon of the Church within a comprehensive theological perspective.

That October the Bologna workshop established contact with a singular personality: Ivan Illich, a priest of Austrian origin who had been transferred to Latin America. This fostered contact between Latin American and European bishops and encouraged the group to consider new horizons:

> We're looking a bit at Fr. Ivan Illich these days. Slavic by origin, he worked with the Puerto Ricans in New York; he was rector of the Catholic University in Puerto Rico, but, having refused to support the national Catholic political party, he was driven away. At this time, he is head of a lay organization that controls much of the financial assistance coming from Catholics in Europe to those in South America. He is in open conflict with Samore, who wants instead to create a typical Roman congregation for South America, but up until now has encountered fierce opposition from the local bishops. Illich, in fact, is in Rome to organize a single conference for all of the conferences of Latin American bishops. Everything is to pass through this body. He is willing to buy the technical assistance that we can sell him on behalf of his bishops, who, unlike the Italians, know what they don't know. He is as sharp a man as Dossetti, with less scholarly training, but with fewer monastic inhibitions and a better business sense.[4]

The Responsibilities of the Bishops and the Unity of the Churches

With the crisis over *De Ecclesia* behind them, the Council began discussing the schema relating to the functions and powers of the bishops. The previous April the fathers had received a text that combined a group of preparatory schemata dealing with the bishops' responsibilities in leading the dioceses, their relationship with the central Roman authorities, the bishops' conferences, and the territorial assets of the Churches (dioceses and parishes). In spite of a number of revisions, the document still showed the influence of a vertical conception of the Church, which obscured the local, territorial dimension. It was, nevertheless, accepted by the assembly as the basis for the Council's later work.

The most interesting point of this discussion concerned the bishops' management of a single territory, usually a nation, through the episcopal conferences. These bodies, which had already been formed in some parts of the Church, grouped together the bishops of a single geographical, linguistic, and political area. This permitted them to form a common pastoral strategy and to face their problems from a number of points of view and with more resources to devote to their commonly adopted solutions. The question facing the Council was that of giving these conferences a real and proper juridical status, granting them a broad field of activity that would limit Roman centralism, and equipping them with enough power so they would be able to exercise a true leadership role. In essence, the question of empowering the bishops' conferences was another manifestation of the theme of the relationship between the bishops and the pope. It was, in the end, proposing a form of decentralization and the collegial exercise of authority, although this was limited in geographical terms.

This topic, like others that involved the question of the relationship between the bishops and the Roman Curia, was linked with the somewhat sensitive question of the reform of the Curia. Originally a purely executive body, since the end of the 1500s the Curia had gradually assumed roles of decision and initiative. Although its powers were always formally sanctioned by the authority of the pope, in reality it frequently determined and conditioned the will of the pontiff himself. The scope of its powers was such that it was able to oppose any conception of the Church that did not limit itself to the reaffirmation of its monarchical structure, which the Council had just laid to rest.

But would the Council be able to address the question of the reform of the Curia? This was a particularly thorny question after the speech by Paul VI on September 21, in which, on the eve of the resumption of the Council, he had outlined the course he planned to follow for the reform of this same body. At most, the Council would be able to give advice to the extent it was asked to do so; this was the opinion of some fairly authoritative fathers, for whom the reform of the Curia was not to be addressed in the schema under discussion because this did not seem to be the proper place for it.

But more than the individual topics under discussion, what characterized this period was the constant presence of a substantial tension related to the voting that had taken place on October 30. The secret opposition that had delayed the voting now came to the surface, denying the value of the vote. Because the vote had been presented as a sort of opinion poll, the opposition tried to empty it of any kind of value or consequence, as if the Theological Commission could proceed without taking it into account.

On November 8 Cardinal Frings of Cologne, one of the most influential members of the entire assembly, intervened in the discussion to ask whether the vote on the college of bishops taken October 30 could be completely ignored in spite of the fact that it expressed the almost unanimous outlook of the fathers. To the applause of the bishops, he added, "[The Holy Office's] manner of conducting itself, on many counts, is no longer in keeping with our age, is harmful to the Church, and is a cause of scandal for many." (It was to the authority of the Holy Office that the Theological Commission had appealed.) It must be added, Frings continued, that no one should be condemned before being heard and being given the opportunity to correct himself. This was the sentiment of many, and had at last been expressed in the solemn Council hall, where an atmosphere of freedom and frankness was increasingly widespread.

Shortly after this Archbishop Eugene D'Souza of India brought the Roman Curia into question again, describing it as a "centralized power" unfit for modern times. He called for precise limitations on its powers and the granting to the bishops of all the faculties required for their task, asking, "Are bishops still not old enough to resolve the questions that arise in their territories?" His remark drew sustained applause. A few minutes later, seized by deep emotion and in a choked voice, Cardinal Ottaviani, the head of the Holy Office and president of the Theological Commission, before reading from his prepared text, responded to the accusations of Cardinal Frings of Cologne, registering "a most vigorous protest against the words that have been spoken against the Supreme Congregation of the Holy Office, whose head is the supreme pontiff." Then he added, "Whoever wants to be one of Christ's sheep must be led to pasture by Peter. It is not the sheep that must guide Peter, but Peter who must guide the sheep."

Ottaviani concluded by saying that the October 30 vote did not mean anything; that it was only a proposal on the part of the Council that the Theological Commission must decide upon, because it was this commission that had been appointed to decide upon questions of faith and custom. His expansive view of the commission's power would have transformed his commission from a technical instrument for the preparation of texts into a decision-making body of the Council. Following his logic, could other commissions not function in the same way? It is significant that the English Benedictine Abbot Butler maintained that Ottaviani's reply, by identifying the pope with the Holy Office, had "attributed to the pope methods that are against natural law."

This battle of words received significant media coverage and was interpreted as the test of the new atmosphere that had been created in the Catholic Church. The result of this was an increased bitterness in the relationship between the majority and the minority in the assembly. An even more serious blow came from the criticism voiced by Italy's Bishop Carli on November 13, in which he brought into doubt the legitimacy of appealing to a vote that, according to him, had been conducted abruptly and without respecting rules of order, thereby gravely compromising the stature of the moderators. Angelina Nicora wrote about this situation in her diary:

> Unfortunately, very early we began to fear the manner in which the Curial party would seek, on the one hand, to invalidate the vote, and, on the other, to frighten the pope. In fact, both attacks have already begun. The first of these maintains that the October 30 vote was based upon documents of an uncertain status, because these were created without consulting the Theological Commission, the only one with both knowledge and competency in this matter. That is, an attempt has been made to transform the commissions from technical instruments for the preparation of outlines into directive bodies for the Council. What tedious days we have spent! The moderators, whose authority should have been significantly increased after the success of October 30, have been judged as guilty by insignificant men like Carli, Bishop of Segni, by unintelligent and theologically unequipped men like Siri, by conservative and reactionary men like Ottaviani, Ruffini, and some of the North Americans. North American conservatism has had a lot to say at the Council.
>
> They have also frightened the pope with the specter of the Jansenist *conciliabolo* [pseudo-council] in Pistoia (1786), bringing before him the fear that the same situations would be repeated. In a state of agitation, Fr. Carlo [Colombo] told Pippo Dossetti on Thursday, November 7, that the pope had told him in the course of a conversation, "They even suggested to me that I should close the Council!" The fact that they said this to him is not so important as the fact that he has thought about it enough to mention it to others. During the same conversation he [Paul VI] showed great concern for the doctrinal implications that these matters might have and asked for a summary of the events at Pistoia, which Boris [Ulianich] prepared [in Bologna] from Saturday November 9 to Monday November 11.
>
> After the voting on October 30 the major problem that needed to be faced was that of the replacement of the members of the commissions. The African bishops presented to the pope, the moderators, and the Coordinating Commission an explicit request in this regard (it had been drawn up by Pippo [Dossetti]). This request repeated an

earlier one made by Cardinal Lercaro during his first address, when he asked that the men who had shown themselves to be the most prepared in regard to the problems under discussion should be called to participate in the respective commissions.[5]

The moderators themselves, whose authority should have grown after the results of October 30, were in reality placed in the chair of the accused by an embattled minority, in spite of the comment of Paul VI, who said in regard to the October 30 vote, "We have won!" With some difficulty, the storm blew over. As Dossetti maintained at the time, the situation was so dynamic that all the problems were out on the table. One could change only the order in which they would be addressed; they would keep coming back until they were resolved.

According to Nicora:

> The second half of November was characterized by a struggle between the moderators and the other directive bodies (especially the main Coordinating Commission) over the attempt of the latter gradually to devalue and nullify the October 30 vote. One important event was Lercaro's audience with the pope (at the pope's request) on the morning of Friday (the 15th?). That afternoon, a meeting was to be held among the three directive bodies—the moderators, the Council of Presidents, and the Coordinating Commission—in the presence of the pope. Cardinal Lercaro's secretary had received news of the meeting the evening before but had not told him about it in order to avoid disturbing his sleep. Early the next morning the cardinal wrote a stern letter to the pope, telling him of all the bitterness he felt because of the moderators' complete lack of authority. The audience on the morning [of November 15] was certainly not a very positive one; the cardinal came away sad, and with the impression that there was nothing else that could be done, and at the end of the meeting itself gave to the pope the letter that he had written. From the written version of the pope's remarks, we know that he said that if he had to change the commissions he would also have to change the moderators.[6]

Special attention was given at the Council to a proposal to create a group of bishops around the pope that would assume the functions that had been performed for a few centuries by the consistory of cardinals (analogous to the "permanent" synod that assists the Patriarch of Constantinople). This group would carry out a close and frequent collaboration with the pope on the problems facing the Church as a whole. The proposal was inspired by the desire to lighten the increasingly burdensome papal office with the advice and consent of a representative body of the episcopal college, overcoming the exaggerated isolation of the pope, which had become even more pronounced after Vatican I.

But it was Paul VI himself who later took matters into his own hands. In September 1965 he decided on the establishment of the Synod of Bishops as a representative body of the episcopate with consultative functions in regard to the pope. This would meet every two or three years to formulate proposals on topics that would be decided by the pope himself. This would fulfill one of the significant requests of the bishops, although since they would have no power to make decisions, it would leave unsolved the problem of the exclusively personal dimension of the papal office.

Divergent points of view were also expressed about the wisdom, or lack of it, of increasing the number of titular bishops—bishops named the heads of ancient dioceses no longer in existence—who were intended to help another bishop, and also of setting an age limit for bishops to serve as active bishops. After nine general congregations the project was sent back to the commission for further elaboration. For his part Paul VI wanted to give a sign of his own sensitivity to the bishops' requests for greater recognition of their individual responsibility, and on November 30 he approved a Motu Proprio by which the bishops were recognized as having a number of powers and faculties that in recent centuries had been taken from them and appropriated by Rome.

Discussions on Ecumenism Begin

On November 18 the discussion of the working draft on ecumenism began. The schema had been made available by the mixed commission of the Secretariat for Christian Unity and the Commission for the Oriental Churches. The five chapters sought to present the Catholic principles of ecumenism, the criteria for implementing these principles, the Catholic Church's relationship with the Eastern Orthodox Churches and its less organic relationship with the Churches that sprang from the Protestant Reformation, the significance of the Jewish people in the history of salvation, and finally, the controversial question of religious liberty.

It was obvious that the document sought to elaborate a Catholic attitude toward the problem of the unity of the Churches. It was rooted in the expectations raised by John XXIII and by the presence of non-Catholic observers at the Council. The goal would be to overcome the futile hope of the "return to Rome" of the separated brethren, that is, schismatics (Eastern Orthodox), heretics (Protestants), and Anglicans. The older attitude had not only isolated Catholics from the ecumenical movement, which had made gigantic strides during the twentieth century in binding the different Churches together, but above all it had solidified within the Roman Church a fatalistic, passive acceptance of the division among Christians as an unpleasant but unavoidable reality that was someone else's fault.

The proposed document was received rather favorably for its section on ecumenism, while the sections on relations with the Jews and on religious

Catholic News Service

This picture shows several of the sixty representatives from major Christian denominations who attended Council sessions and whose impact, particularly in informal conversations, was vital to the way many documents were shaped.

liberty became objects of violent opposition. The recognition of the salvific significance of the Jewish people was opposed not only by traditional Catholic anti-Semitism, but also by the Arab or pro-Arab fathers, who feared that such an action would be exploited politically by the Zionists and the aggressive new state of Israel. John XXIII's recent decision to remove from the prayers of the liturgy of Good Friday the mention of the "deicide" on the part of the Jewish people had still not had a deep impact on the Catholic mentality.

The proposal to consider religious liberty not only as an assertion of the rights of the Catholic Church, but also as the recognition of every person's liberty of conscience, raised concerns and profound reservations among various groups at the Council, in part perhaps because of its unsophisticated theological formulation. Nevertheless, on November 21 the schema was approved as a working document and was sent to the commission.

The Mass Belongs to Everybody

This brought to an end the second period of the Council, which culminated in the solemn session of December 4, 1963, during the course of which the Council definitively approved the first two documents of its history: the Constitution on the Sacred Liturgy, *Sacrosanctum Concilium* (with 2,147 votes in favor, 4 against, and 1 abstention) and the Decree on the Means of Social Communication, *Inter Mirifica* (with 1,960 votes in favor). The weakness of the latter document explains the high number (164) of votes against it.

In the end, after an exhausting, seemingly endless series of votes requested by the minority, the impulse toward liturgical reform came to a happy conclusion. The constitution was laid out in an introduction and seven chapters. The most important of these were the first two, which were dedicated to the general principles of reform, the promotion of the liturgy, and the mystery of the Eucharist. With this decision the Council reached the important goal of a long and complex journey: the approval of the active participation of the common faithful at liturgical celebrations. In fact, since the end of the nineteenth century the liturgical movement had involved many of the faithful, as a body, in many areas of the Church, and in the second part of the pontificate of Pius XII this had received its first modest show of support.

In reality, the constitution, in dictating the directives for liturgical renewal, formulated a series of theological and ecclesiological principles (such as the centrality of the word of God and the importance given to the local Church) that were of great significance and had long been left in the shadows. These principles were destined to exercise a positive influence on the entire work of Vatican II.[7]

In view of these two solemn acts of approval, the question was also raised of the formula by which the pope would accept the Council's decisions, conferring upon them juridical authority for the whole Church through an act of promulgation. The Council's rules of order provided for the same formula that Pius IX had used in 1870 at Vatican Council I, when the pope, with the support of the Council's vote *(sacro approbante concilio)*, approved and promulgated the documents. Paul VI was convinced that such a formula was untenable in the light of the new ecclesial mentality of communion that had been expressed by the great majority of the fathers. He accepted a proposal that had been brought forth by a small group of periti—which included a substantial contribution from the Bologna workshop—and on December 4 he used for the first time a formula that he would use from that time on. It was a formula much more consistent with the Council's point of view, according to which, having invoked the Trinity, the pope affirmed that

the items that are found in this constitution, both individually and as whole, have been found agreeable to the Council fathers. And We, with the apostolic authority granted to us by Christ, together with the venerable fathers, also approve, decree, and establish these in the

Holy Spirit, and we ordain that what has been established thus by the Council should be promulgated for the glory of God.

In his speech concluding the work of 1963, Paul VI emphasized the results that had been achieved and the great amount of work still to be done, and warned against impatience and arbitrary initiative in the application of liturgical reform. He also announced his decision to make a pilgrimage to Jerusalem, during which, after centuries of hostile estrangement, he would meet with the Patriarch of Constantinople, Athenagoras. Thus the pope made his own the yearning for unity felt by all Christians. For a pope, going to Jerusalem was an act of humility that acknowledged every Christian's indebtedness to the gospel message and submission to the very origins of the Church.

The definitive approval of the Constitution on the Sacred Liturgy just halfway through the Council ushered in a period of practical acceptance for and application of the Council's decisions. The initiative necessarily passed from the episcopate to the entire Church, and this created new problems that were exhilarating but also fraught with unknown consequences. As in the past, acceptance and application would constitute the incontrovertible proof of the historical validity of the decisions and spirit of the Council. The liturgical constitution marked out the desired path and was able to generate immense energy for the effort to realize a "full and active participation of the entire people" in the liturgy, and thus in the life of the Church.

The New Face of the Council

The recess from 1962 to 1963 had been dominated by harsh and demanding confrontations that took place within the various commissions, and it was made more confusing by the scarcity of information. Nevertheless, at the end of those months it was possible to bring a second preparatory phase to a successful conclusion. It seemed that the Council had found its way, but the long road ahead was to show that even advances that appeared to be perfectly solid could be brought up for discussion again. So it is not improper to look at the beginning of the second period of the Council, at the end of September 1963, as a new beginning that would be marked by two significant factors: the presence of a new bishop of Rome and the effort made during the recess of the Council to move beyond the tendencies that emerged from the period of preparation.

But how were the elements of novelty and continuity balanced during the second period? The balance of papal influence could not help but change in the passage from Roncalli to Martini. Bea and Suenens saw the influence of their advice decrease, and Ottaviani was no longer the watchdog of orthodoxy. Those who saw an increase in their influence, apart from Carlo Colombo of Milan, theological consultant to Paul VI, included Cardinals Döpfner and Ruffini, and Jesuit canon-law specialist Bertrams. These were not overwhelming or radical changes, but their importance would increase. In the new balance of influence Secretary of State Cardinal Cicognani also made a successful bid for greater weight as president of the Coordinating Commission.

The novelty at the summit of the Council's leadership was supplied by the creation of the college of moderators at the behest of Pope Paul. This definitively sidelined the unwieldy Council of Presidents, which had had little to show for itself in 1962. But one gets the impression that the moderators fluctuated between the extremes of serving as a sort of windshield protecting the pope from the gales of the assembly and of actually guiding the Council, which had frequently seemed to be rudderless.

The influence of the assembly commissions gradually increased as the Council increased its work and expressed tendencies different from the ones that had dominated during the formulation of the schemata. It was indispensable that those schemata be revised or re-created. In any case, the commissions, which had been elected during the first days of an inexperienced assembly and headed by the presiding members of the corresponding congregations of the Curia, did not succeed in harmonizing themselves with the new points of view that emerged in the assembly. In November 1962 one of the rounds of voting had resulted in the relegation to minority status of one of the doctrinal schemata presented by the Theological Commission. Hundreds of the bishops found themselves unexpectedly converging on these topics. During the Council's second phase this convergence would be expressed in crucial views on the concept of the Church. This convergence would become the majority viewpoint.

In October and November 1963 the assembly at Vatican II would live through some intense moments because of the choices it had to make and the tension that these choices would generate. The laborious experience of the first phase—including the difficulty of ordering and pruning the schemata still awaiting the Council's attention and the fundamental impulse to refurbish the image of the Church—made many long for a drastic summarization of all the schemata within the document *De Ecclesia* (except for *De Liturgia*, which was almost ready). From another point of view, the Döpfner Plan for a conscientious conclusion to the Council's work, inspired by Paul VI in the summer of 1963 and then elaborated by the Cardinal of Munich, had to come to grips with the widespread desire that this conscientious conclusion take place before the end of 1964.

The votes of October 30, which had been suspended for two whole weeks by a senseless battle within the Council's leadership and had then been bitterly criticized by the minority, undeniably constituted a liberating turn of events. But the Council understood that the renewal of the Church's doctrine, as crucial as it was, would be fruitless by itself. The developing awareness of this definitely alarmed the circles that had counted on the Council to follow conservative positions. They tried to make Pope Paul VI share in their anxieties in order to make up for the followers they had lost at the assembly. Thus the second phase of the Council and the second interval between sessions were marked by pressure on Paul VI to rein in the tendencies of the majority.

At the end of the second session Vatican II formally emerged from its long phase of gestation—which had risked becoming impotent—through its definitive approval of two documents: *Sacrosanctum Concilium*, the constitution on liturgical renewal, and *Inter Mirifica*, the decree on the media.

The Constitution on the Sacred Liturgy, which was designed as a set of guidelines, began a movement for renewal inspired by the active participation of the community of the faithful in liturgical celebrations, which were asserted to be the summit of the Church's life. There were some other important doctrinal perspectives—for example, the centrality of the Eucharist—that might have remained in the shadows. Vatican II was working on ground that had already been prepared, though it was still constrained by habits dominated by a devastating "rubricism." The effect of *Sacrosanctum Concilium* upon the foundations of the Church was direct and immediate. Liturgical renewal was awaited and received widespread interest. The cautionary passages inserted within the Council document itself could not stop many ecclesial communities from making the Council's decision their own and putting it into practice without delay.

But the assimilation of the Council's next work was difficult, slow, and ultimately unsatisfying. By this I refer to the significance for renewal of the understanding of the Church as the community or the home of all the faithful, which was contained within the goals of liturgical reform.

Resolving the difficulty of how the pope was to implement the Council's decrees, Paul VI made a good choice in his formula for approving and promulgating the Council's decisions. It was based upon proposals from the assembly. The formula hinged upon the idea of the pope's agreement with the conclusions voted upon by the assembly. This constituted the high point of convergence between Pope Paul and the Council majority. With this formulation the relationship between the pope and the Council superseded the long medieval and modern period during which this relationship had increasingly become one that accented their differences, when it was not one of absolute estrangement. As articulated, with the pope promulgated the Council's decisions as his own laws, adding the formula *sacro approbante concilio* (with the sacred Council approving).

The most prominent international event during the weeks of the second phase was the assassination of U.S. President John F. Kennedy on November 22, 1963, which was felt deeply within Vatican II. There was also the stormy period in Algeria as France withdrew its last troops on June 14, 1964. Also troubling was the worsening of the Vietnam conflict following increased U.S. involvement, in spite of growing resistance from domestic public opinion. All these events affected the atmosphere of the Council, whose work did not take place in isolation.

The growing political opposition in the Arab world toward the Council's eventual consideration of the question of Jewish-Christian relations drew widespread support among the bishops who came from Arab countries. They were accompanied by the Vatican Secretary of State in their resistance toward a document on the Jews *(De Judaeis)*. And there was another situation in which the immense transformations taking place in Africa were noted by the Council. Africa had initially been represented by a group of mainly European "missionary" bishops, but a growing number of indigenous bishops, African through and through, steadily began to emerge.

The Council was also living in a new condition of openness toward the media, which had overcome the reigning climate of exclusion found in the previous year. The Council was no longer hidden away in secret. This was a new atmosphere that not only fostered a more ample and correct diffusion of information to the public, but also permitted a more tranquil exchange between journalists and members of the Council in regard to world events.

The emotional announcement of the pope's pilgrimage to Jerusalem surprised and exhilarated the Council. It is difficult to deny that this announcement was an outcome of Vatican II. It would have been almost impossible to imagine such a decision apart from the change in direction brought about by Pope John and the meeting of the Council. In any case, it is certain that Paul VI formed the idea for this trip immediately after his election and then planned it as the ingenious first act of his pontificate. This pilgrimage was situated within the context of the new approach brought about by Vatican II. As an indication of the depth of this new orientation, the meeting with the Patriarch of Constantinople, Athenagoras, was at the center of the entire event. The original spiritual inspiration of the visit was transfigured into an act of communion of the highest value and of undeniable ecumenical ratifications. The consequences would be seen even within Vatican II itself, when, at the beginning of the third working session in the autumn of 1964, the observers sent by Patriarch Athenagoras would finally arrive in Rome. Before the pope's visit to Jerusalem, they had been awaited in vain.

The creation on January 25, 1964, of the "Council for the implementation of the liturgical constitution," which the Council itself had requested and which had been quickly approved by Paul VI, was an authentic anticipation of the post-Council period:

In his Thursday [October 10, 1963] audience with the four moderators, the pope handed over to them some folders containing various topics. We were greatly reassured by the fact that the pope told our representative [Lercaro] that once the schema on the liturgy had been approved, he wanted Lercaro to provide a written decree for the immediate implementation of what had been decided. This was because Larraona [the head of the Roman Congregation for Rites] was saying it would be at least a decade before application would be possible.[8]

After the approval of the liturgical constitution it was indispensable that guidelines be produced for the interpretation of this document, which might be conditioned, for example, by the translation of the liturgical books into the various languages. The conciliar constitution itself had assigned a great deal of responsibility to the individual bishops and to the episcopal conferences, but it seemed indispensable that both of these have a point of reference at the Holy See.

It also seemed impossible to propose that this point of reference be the Congregation of Rites in the Roman Curia, because it had systematically resisted the development of the Constitution on the Sacred Liturgy. This explains the satisfaction that met the courageous decision of Paul VI, all the more so because two famous liturgists, Cardinal Lercaro and Fr. Bugnini, both of whom had repeatedly demonstrated their commitment to renewal, were appointed to the *Consilium*, which would act as the point of reference. In the spring of 1964 this *Consilium* appeared to be the model of the bodies that would coordinate postconciliar activities. In the event, however, the *Consilium* remained just an isolated case and was quickly reabsorbed into the corresponding congregation.

In spite of their uncertainties and limitations, the second period and the second recess constituted a development of Vatican II and of Catholic self-awareness that had been unimaginable just a few years before. By the beginning of the autumn of 1964, the Council had passed the halfway point. Five years had passed since its announcement in 1959. The hypothesis of a brief council had been demolished, and the fears that the announcement had raised had been deflated; an image emerged of Vatican II as a "new" council, as a chance for renewal. And yet an impression also arose that the results might not be completely satisfying.

4

The Church Is a Communion
(1964)

Halfway There

There was still a great deal of work to be done after the conclusion of the
second period. In mid-April 1964 the Coordinating Commission had before it a dozen projects that had already been reviewed by the respective
commissions and were waiting to be sent to the fathers for preliminary
examination. Some of them were particularly dear to the bishops' hearts
and already represented a commitment for the Council in the eyes of public opinion: the documents on the Church, on revelation, on ecumenism,
and the one on relations between the Church and the world, which had
not yet been presented in the hall.

There were two other projects, both eagerly awaited but rife with difficulties—the schemata on religious liberty and on the Jewish people. By
now these had been formulated as declarations in themselves rather than
as chapters in the document on ecumenism. Finally, there was a group of
projects less interesting in public opinion but of great pastoral importance;
these would essentially depend upon the theological point of view that
would be found in the Constitution on the Church. These were the document on the bishops and the governing of dioceses, and others that were
not yet known to the fathers on priests—on the laity, on mission, on the
religious, on the Eastern Churches, and others.

In spite of the drastic reduction in the number of the schemata that had
taken place at the beginning of 1963, the Council continued to suffer from
the excessive and disorganized activity of the period of preparation. This
had a particular effect upon this third period of the Council's work, which
frequently moved at a frantic pace, so much so that jokes were made about
the Council fathers' "Olympic marathon." As shown in part by this excess
in the day's order of business, the central problem considered during the
recess that took place between the winter of 1963 and the autumn of 1964
was that of the duration of the Council and the things that were impeding

its conclusion. Work, it was concluded, had to be organized more efficiently to permit completing it.

As for the duration of the Council, there was talk of the inclination of Paul VI to conclude the work definitively at the end of the next period, which was scheduled to begin on September 14, 1964. Various arguments of a practical nature seemed to support this idea, particularly the difficulties that the bishops faced in remaining away from their churches. This especially affected the bishops of the poorest and most remote continents. But neither was it irrelevant that the Council represented a moment of exceptional dynamism in the life of the Church, which could not help but disturb the daily administration of work of the Curial offices, which hoped for a "return to normality." But the breadth and complexity of the problems still to be considered argued for the continuation of the Council. In particular, there was the argument that, given its nature, the Council needed to find its own rhythm and its own point of completion. Some brought up the hypothesis of a long recess (lasting as long as several years) that would permit assimilation and a series of experiments prior to the definitive formulation of decisions for reform.

A few changes in the rules of order provided for greater efficiency in the working procedures. In order to decrease the number of speeches, the moderators would have the ability to call together the fathers scheduled to speak on the same topic to delegate one or two of them to speak in the name of the entire group. Furthermore, in order to speak after the close of a debate, one now needed to represent at least seventy bishops, not five. Also, a summary of each speech needed to be presented not three but five days ahead of time, and the previously exempt cardinals were now made subject to this rule.

Instead of the hoped-for renewal of membership in the commissions, only a few members were added to each of these, some of them elected and some of them nominated by the pope. As it turned out, this was only a palliative measure, unable to overcome the "disconnect" between the viewpoints of the Council majority and those of the majorities within the commissions. Nicora wrote:

> The atmosphere is heavy, and at this moment there is a sense of disappointment over the new measures to be taken with the commissions, which seem neither to produce nor to promise any real change. What will these new members be able to do? It is known that at the commission [for the bishops and the government of dioceses] headed by Cardinal Marella, which is not even one of the worst, not even the nomination of a third vice-president has taken place. Marella maintained that the excellent results produced by the two already in place made the nomination of a new one pointless. It seems that no one wanted to raise his hand in order to speak, and certainly not in favor of the nomination, and thus the meeting was adjourned.[1]

Although these changes in the regulations did lead to a certain increase in efficiency, they also made it more difficult to have a true debate in the Council. The need to present a summary of one's speech five days before delivering it meant that speeches were never perfectly in tune with the discussion under way. The absurd result of this was that the addresses of a general nature, which made an overall assessment of problems rather than presenting individual proposals, fell into the greatest disuse, because the Council could never initiate a discussion about them, and the commissions found in them no proposals for the modification of any points in the documents.

The interest raised by the Council and the formation of organized pressure groups resulted in the production of "minor" writings, which their proponents tried to distribute to the bishops as they entered St. Peter's. The directive bodies of the Council, and especially the secretariat, made a serious effort to block the distribution of any unauthorized document in the hall or its immediate vicinity in order to avoid undue pressure upon the fathers. But the root of the problem was the lack of places where the themes of the Council could be discussed in a more direct manner and with the involvement of the periti and other experts. The experiment at the Council of Trent whereby the Council fathers, before the actual sessions of the Council, attended meetings at which specialists in various areas of theology conducted a frank doctrinal debate was, unfortunately, not repeated at Vatican II. This left more room for the erratic influence of the mass media and the various circles that formed spontaneously.

The groups of bishops met with each other based on language, but early on even the secretaries of the episcopal conferences met together from time to time. At the initiative of Brazilian Archbishop Geraldo de Proença Sigaud and with the support of French Archbishop Marcel Lefebvre, beginning in October 1964 weekly meetings were held of the Coetus Internationalis Patrum, the point of reference for the fathers in the minority. During these meetings they debated the topics under discussion at the Council, prepared amendments, and prepared the strategy that they would follow in their work, "always following the traditional doctrine of the Church."

Not only bishops met in language groups. An influential discussion circle was the International Documentation and Communication Center (IDOC), promoted by a Dutch group. In addition, the so-called Belgian team, which gathered together many French-speaking bishops and theologians at the Belgian college, was of considerable importance. This group was coordinated by Albert Prignon and conducted by Suenens. A certain influence was also exercised by the Bologna workshop, which assembled around Lercaro and Dossetti. And during the interval between the second and third sessions of the Council, the publication by Paul VI of the encyclical *Ecclesiam Suam* on August 6, 1963, focused attention again upon the conception of the Church, and also on the relationship between the Church and the modern world.

1964: An Overbooked Agenda

The solemn session of September 14, 1964, was inaugurated with a Mass concelebrated by Paul VI and twenty-four of the fathers. It was a symbolic expression of the liturgical renewal promoted by the constitution approved a few months earlier. The observers finally included the delegates of the Patriarch of Constantinople (and of other Orthodox and Nestorian Churches). Their participation was clearly the fruit of the Jerusalem meeting between Paul VI and Athenagoras. Relations between Rome and Constantinople had been intensified especially through the untiring work of Fr. Pierre Duprey of the Secretariat for Christian Unity and the Romanian Orthodox monk André Scrima, who enjoyed the trust of Patriarch Athenagoras.

In his speech the pope reaffirmed the Church's need to define itself and the urgency of expressing in its fullness the doctrine that Vatican Council I had formulated in an incomplete way, concentrating only on the pope's prerogatives. But it was clear that he was concerned about preventing the doctrine of episcopal collegiality from implying any reversal of the doctrine on papal prerogatives approved almost a century before.

In making these concerns his own, Paul VI, although he confirmed his openness to the doctrine of episcopal collegiality, also placated the Council minority, which was inflexibly hostile toward the image of the Church as a communion. The difficulties and tensions that would afflict the atmosphere and work of this entire third period were already present in embryonic form. But these were fleshless phantoms, because no one among the great majority in the Council that was fighting for an exhaustive definition of the nature and functions of the episcopacy had ever expressed or implied any lessened fidelity to papal primacy. The obstinacy of the opponents of collegiality gave the impression that they had created, or were trying to create, a sort of psychosis of fear, as if collegiality could overshadow papal primacy or create friction between the college of bishops and its head, the pope. This despite the fact that speakers repeatedly affirmed that there is no episcopal college apart from union with its head, the pope, and that the possibility of autonomous initiative on the part of the college was not admitted. But this did not appease those who, forgetful of the uninterrupted historical tradition and especially of the divine origin of the apostolic college, attributed to the proponents of collegiality nonexistent "democratic tendencies" or a "surrender to the fashions of the day," not to speak of a diminished fidelity to doctrine.

Because of the above mentioned matters, when the Council reopened in the autumn of 1964 there were clouds on the horizon. Despite their overwhelming majority, the fathers who emphasized collegiality would contend with preoccupations of the minority, which probably did not make up as much as 10 percent of the assembly. One might make the case that this great effort by the Council served to make its formulation of such an important truth as precise, deliberate, and clear as it could be. But it is not possible to escape the impression that the formulation of this doctrine did not take place so much as part of a faithful search for the truth about the divine origin and functions of the episcopal college as it did in the context of ill-defined but persistent anxieties caused by shadows that created almost insuperable difficulties for the project.

On July 7, 1964, the fathers were informed that they would be working on three documents that they had already discussed extensively the year before: *De Ecclesia* (On the Church), *De Oecumenismo* (On Ecumenism), and *De Episcoporum Munere* (On the Office of Bishops). There were also three other schemata to be worked on: on revelation, on the apostolate of the laity, and on the Church in the modern world. From September 16 to September 30 the fathers began examining again the schema on the Church. After the debates of October 1963, the commission, especially through the efforts of the additional new secretary, [Louvain-educated] Gérard Philips, had completed a document expounded in eight chapters. To the original four chapters (on the mystery of the Church, on the people of God, on the hierarchical structure of the Church, and on the laity) were added sections on the universal call to holiness, on religious life, on the eschatological horizon of the Church, and on the Virgin Mary. The first two chapters were approved without significant resistance, while through the initiative of the minority the third chapter was divided into thirty-nine sections, each of which had to be voted on separately.

During the Council's discussions on September 21, one authoritative exponent of the Holy Office, Pietro Parente, unexpectedly declared himself in favor of the principle of episcopal collegiality, referring to research by the Bologna workshop published a few months before on the development of doctrine on authority in the universal Church from the sixteenth to the nineteenth centuries.[2] On January 26, 1965, as recorded by Angelina Nicora, I—the author of that document—was summoned by Paul VI:

> Pino [Alberigo] went for his audience; he returned, beaming, at 12:40. More than cordial, the pope was affectionate; I get the impression that Pino was rather won over by him: he spoke to me of his penetrating eyes. The pope welcomed him as Pippo's [Dossetti's] successor as director of the center. They spoke of the work of what the pope calls the "aristocratic" center. "Is that a reprimand, your Holiness?" [Alberigo asked], just to get rid of any clouds. But it wasn't a reprimand. The pope wants him to respond to reviews of the book; he invoked the Holy Spirit upon the overseers of his [university] studies. He approved the document *De Ecclesia* [from the project of supplementary documentation] and asked that it be released before the fourth session. They spoke for twenty minutes, in the form of a dialogue. Pino made to him a clear profession of faith in papal primacy,

saying that the thing that troubled him the most was that some had put this in doubt.[3]

Exhausting voting sessions were held from September 21 to September 30 in an attempt to break down the cohesion of the majority. The most consistent opposition was raised against episcopal collegiality, which received more than 300 votes against, and the institution of the permanent diaconate, with more than 600. The possibility of conferring the diaconate without imposing the obligation of celibacy was rejected, with 1,364 votes against. When the time finally came to vote on chapter III of *De Ecclesia* as a whole, there were only 42 votes against it, while there were 572 votes of approval with reservations (*placet iuxta modum*). The minority was hoping to whittle away bit by bit the document on collegiality. The dominating factor here, as on other occasions of voting, was the desire of Paul VI to attain unanimity in the approval of the schema.

The last chapter, the one on the Virgin Mary, also faced opposition. To the fathers most involved in Marian piety, the insertion of this chapter into the Constitution on the Church seemed like a minimalistic solution, even in terms of the high number of requests for real and proper mariological definitions that had been made during the pre-preparatory consultation. But the majority found the chapter to be a satisfactory solution, one that expressed an understanding held by the entire Church—and even beyond the confines of Roman Catholicism—while not expressing the opinions of a few schools of thought or the devotional excesses of certain groups.

On September 18 examination of the document on the bishops and the governing of the dioceses began. The way in which this topic was interwoven with the development of the document *De Ecclesia* brought a delicate problem to light. The schema on the bishops, which was of a more directly pastoral and reformist nature, depended upon the theological expression found in documents on more general topics, as did those on the apostolate of the laity, on priests, and on the Eastern Churches. It was inevitable that the doctrinal orientations contained in the document on the Church would form the basis for considering the function of the bishops, just as it would be impossible to speak of the laity without going back to the part of that same document dealing with the people of God.

But *De Ecclesia* had still not received definite approval, and this permitted the fathers in the minority to propose again the fundamental points of their conception of the Church. This is precisely what Bishop Carli did in regard to episcopal collegiality and the bishops' participation in the leadership of the universal Church. As he did not accept that by episcopal consecration the bishop becomes part of the episcopal college and receives responsibility toward the entire Church—"universal jurisdiction"—he rejected one of the theses underpinning the schema on the bishops, which saw them as participating with the pope in the leadership of the Church as a whole.

This helps to explain how difficult it was to formulate schemata involving the implementation of theological principles before they had been definitively approved and really begun to be part of the Church's life. The Council inevitably began drifting toward compromise texts lacking a rigorous application of the principles of renewal that were supposed to inspire them. In spite of the fact that the majority was in favor of them, the Council still did not have the formal authority, and perhaps not even the effective capacity, to implement such principles. To this should be added a very specific detail (one no less serious for that reason): the great theological themes obviously polarized the part of the Council that was most strenuously involved in questions of doctrine, so much so that this group lacked sufficient resources to apply itself to these "organizational" texts.

In any case, the consideration of the working document on the bishops concluded on September 22 with its being sent back to the commission. The next day the assembly passed to a much thornier matter, examining the document on religious liberty, which was presented with great passion by Bishop De Smedt of Belgium. The level of excitement concerning this topic was particularly strong among the bishops from countries characterized by religious and confessional pluralism, like the United States, where there was still mistrust of the Catholic attitude on the principles of the constitution. A clear acceptance of religious liberty would put and end to such doubts.

The first problem was the title of the document. *Freedom* seemed too reckless a word to some, but to most the word *tolerance* seemed outdated. But the problem was resolved, and the debate was on. The knottiest problem was that of finding a convincing theological formulation of the Church's defense of religious liberty, one that would go beyond the realm of natural law. And this should mean religious liberty not just for Catholics, but for all people, as Cardinal Cushing of the United States hoped. It was a discussion destined to mark the end of an era, a renunciation of the centuries-old attempt to defend the faith, seen as threatened by modern science and culture, by means of state protection. Many hoped that this would eliminate the widespread opinion that the Church was an enemy of freedom.

During the discussion the greatest opposition came from the Italian and Spanish bishops, who were still living in an atmosphere of state protection (through concordats) and who feared the loss of privileges for their churches. The discussion ended on September 25, after an address given by Fr. Carlo Colombo, which was important in that he was the theological consultant to the former Cardinal Montini. He responded to the concerns of the fathers who were afraid of damaging or diminishing the truth of Christian revelation by taking a position in favor of religious liberty. The truth of the gospel, he maintained, communicates itself to all people through its own power and flourishes precisely in an atmosphere of freedom. Polish Archbishop Karol Wojtyla also spoke out in favor of the principle, seeing in the affirmation of religious liberty a significant refutation of the oppression of the communist regime. The schema would not return to the hall until November 19, just before the next recess.

Analogous difficulties faced the project for the declaration on the Jews, which Jesuit Cardinal Bea presented on September 25 in a revision that was significantly toned down in comparison to the one discussed in 1963. There immediately emerged a majority intent upon restoring the original document in all of its vigor. But it encountered significant political interference instigated by both Jewish organizations and Arab countries, traditionally opposed to the Jews. The political authorities of these countries applied pressure to the bishops in their territories, implying that they would find it difficult to exercise their pastoral ministry. As a result, the main preoccupation was with reaffirming the purely religious character of the declaration and preventing it from becoming a political tool in any way. Cardinal Lercaro made a special effort in this direction. Transcending obligatory attitudes by his humanitarian concern for making amends for the Jewish Holocaust, he brought to light the fundamental religious bonds between Jews and Christians—that is, in the Bible and the paschal mystery, both of which, although in different ways, are the witnesses and the zealous guardians. Lercaro emphasized how the reassessment of the word of God and the paschal meal, which had been accomplished by the Constitution on the Sacred Liturgy, gave rise to the need to modify the Church's relationship with the Jewish people. In the end this document was also sent back to the commission to be improved.

Between September 30 and October 6 the Council examined the new document on divine revelation prepared by a mixed commission. This did not give rise to a particularly wide debate, in spite of the fact that the minority maintained that it was not in line with the Council of Trent's

Catholic News Service

The three periti pictured above, Ives Congar, OP, John Courtney Murray, SJ, and Henri de Lubac, SJ, had great influence upon the drafting of documents on mission, the Church, and religious liberty.

decree on scripture and tradition. It was, instead, an integration and development of that decree, according to the intention of the leading theologians who had collaborated on the creation of the new document (Philips, Ratzinger, Congar, and Rahner). The schema obtained wide approval from the majority, but it would not return before the assembly until 1965.

A "Black Week"

Beginning in October 1964 the pace of the Council's work gradually increased, to the point of becoming frantic. This was not only because of the great quantity of documents to be examined, but also because of the variety of arguments that the fathers had to face, each of which required profound rethinking. On another level there were faint but unmistakable symptoms of a weakening of the harmony between the pope and the Council. This was caused in part by Montini's definitive assumption of his new responsibilities and in part by the growing intensity and frequency of the pressure exerted upon him by the most powerful members of the Curia and by the Council minority.

On October 5 the schema on ecumenism returned to the general assembly. In spite of the fact that it had met with widespread agreement, it remained buried under an avalanche of requests for amendments, nearly two thousand of them, which made it necessary to send it back to the commission for more work. The next day the schema on the apostolate of the laity was presented. Unfortunately, the text had not been revised, as might have been hoped, to reflect the second chapter of the schema on the Church, which dealt with the people of God and asserted that all Christians received a permanent apostolic task in baptism. Thus it was inevitable that the document on the laity would be the object of serious criticism, because it maintained that the apostolic task of the laity depended upon a mandate from the hierarchy and conceived of this duty as a way of compensating for the inability of clergy to be present in all areas of society because of secularization and dechristianization. The Council fathers, for their part, wanted to acknowledge the freedom of the people of God to express themselves and to choose their own forms of association in historical and cultural contexts.

Many Council fathers were convinced that even the most widespread and proven lay organizations, like Catholic Action, were not the only models for the future. Conferring this exclusivity upon them brought the risk of locking in and generalizing the responses that had arisen in very specific historical and social situations. When on October 13 the first lay man, Patrick Keegan, was permitted to speak at the conciliar discussions, it was no accident that he asked for a closer connection between the chapter on the people of God in *De Ecclesia* and the document on the apostolate of the laity, inviting the assembly to refrain from limiting the varieties of the lay apostolate through excessively detailed prescriptions. On this basis the document was sent back to the commission for further elaboration. But there was a widespread lack of trust concerning this project. In Bologna, it was expressed this way:

> We have always had reason to shake our heads at the choice of lay people to sit in the Council. It is a lay Curia, whose members are chosen for their station in life rather than for any real competence that might on rare occasions make them capable of collaboration. In the end, the hierarchy does not want competent lay people. This is the problem; it does not get along with them well, and it is afraid of them. Dossetti says that the only one of the lay people that he thinks has been well chosen is Veronese, for whom he prepared on Saturday a magnificent speech on the laity. I hope that Pino [Alberigo] will be able to get a copy of it, but he has told me with that it is really the schema of a treaty. But now it seems that the only one to speak will be Guitton, who ought to be a sort of a harmless, token lay person. So Veronese will not make his speech, or perhaps he will do so at the end of this discussion on *De Ecclesia*, but even that is rather improbable. In any case it is clear that, as Pippo has always maintained, theology has not reached the point of being able to formulate this argument, and so it doesn't need to be discussed, at least not in this session. The best thing would be for the session to be closed right now and then reopened in a few years, but . . . no one has the courage to do this.
>
> Besides, it seems that the members of the Curial party are doing everything they can to raise problems for the pope, one thing after another and each more serious and complicated than the last. They're sure that by doing this they can make him lose his sense of direction and send him reeling. But Pippo [Dossetti] is right when he says that there's no need to get concerned about it, because the situation is so dynamic that if there is resistance at one point, instead of worrying one should simply look for a point of lesser resistance. Anyway, the same problems will come up again in a few years.[4]

Two days later in the assembly it became known that Cardinal Bea had been informed by the General Secretary of the Council that, at the decision of the Coordinating Commission, the draft declaration on relations with the Jews would be inserted into the second chapter of the schema on the Church, where this dealt with relations with non-Christians. The most immediate consequence of this unexpected decision was that the controversial topic passed from the competence of the Secretariat for Christian Unity to that of the Theological Commission. Representatives of the Council majority reacted strongly, and on October 11 a letter signed by seventeen cardinals was sent to Paul VI, asking him that "the rights of the Council [be] respected, and that it be permitted to carry out its work normally."

This action, which was reinforced by a conversation held on October 13 between the pope and Cardinal Frings, had the effect of calming the atmosphere and restoring the previous situation.

The week of November 14, the last week prior to the recess, was the week that authoritative commentators at the time referred to as the *settimana nera* (Black Week). One did, in fact, receive the impression that there was a desire to slow down the pace of renewal that the Council had kept since the beginning and to limit the capacity for initiative that the assembly had laboriously created during its first two years. The fathers had received a folder containing the text of chapter III, on the hierarchical structure (the pope and the bishops), of *De Ecclesia*. With this was included, "by the mandate of the Supreme Authority" (that is, the pope) a "preliminary interpretive note" *(Nota explicative praevia)*. There had been rumors of this for a few days, but it had been prepared in absolute secrecy during the sessions of the Theological Commission, to which only the bishops on the commission had been admitted. Their theologians had been kept out.

The note was presented as an interpretation of the chapter under consideration, submitted to the fathers by the Theological Commission before proceeding to the vote on the amendments. In reality, what was involved was the pope's concern to keep the arguments of the Council minority in view and thus to seek formulations that would produce unanimity during the final vote. With this in mind, Paul VI was proposing a series of amendments to the commission, some of which were accepted and some of which were dropped. It is also true that the rules of order did not provide any specific means for the pope to make contributions to the Council's work, so all his contributions were invested with a sense of authority that disturbed the Council, invoking an image of a deceptive, "monarchical" abuse of power, that deformed the correct model of [exercising] papal primacy.

The note, which was formally signed by Secretary General Archbishop Felici, contained four points plus a *Nota bene*. The first point maintained that the term *college* was not to be understood in a "strictly juridical" sense. It did not, that is, refer to a group of equals. It also maintained that the parallelism between Peter and the other apostles, on the one hand, and the pope and the bishops, on the other, did not imply a relationship of "equality," but a more modest relationship of "proportionality."

The second point insisted that inclusion in the college as an effect of episcopal consecration was conditioned by the "hierarchical communion" (an expression foreign to the theological tradition coined for the occasion) of the new bishop with the pope and the other bishops. It was affirmed that in any case it was the pope's responsibility to make the "juridical determination" of the area (usually a diocese) in which the newly consecrated bishop would exercise his authority.

The third point was dedicated to the relationship between the personal model (the pope by himself) and the collegial model (the pope together with the college of bishops) of exercising supreme authority in the Church. Care was taken to reserve to the pope the freedom to choose one model or the other.

Finally, the fourth point—perhaps the most intricate and contorted of them all—again stressed the pope's freedom from constraint on the part of the episcopal college, and the impossibility of the college itself doing anything without the participation or, at a minimum, the [subsequent] approval of the pope. The brief postscript was motivated by a concern to avoid the impression that there was any desire to negate the role of the bishop and the lawfulness or validity of actions undertaken by the bishops of Eastern Orthodox Churches.

The awkward formulation of the document created problems more difficult than the ones it had been intended to prevent. The note appeared to be a mosaic composed of propositions taken, often word for word, from interventions made at the Council by the leaders of the minority. In spite of this, the document concluded, in part by needlessly repeating what chapter III of *De Ecclesia* had already affirmed. Over time, the proposals it advanced—with the intention of reducing the impact of the conciliar document—were inevitably consigned to irrelevance, because the Council was never required to vote on the contents of the *Nota*.

The assembly's response was not favorable. I was personally sent by Cardinal Lercaro to spend the afternoon of November 15 with Joseph Ratzinger, theological consultant to Cardinal Frings, to examine the possibility of Frings's speaking against the *Nota* in the Council hall. The doctrine of episcopal collegiality had not been some sort of snap decision. Instead, it had been undertaken with deliberation, by means of an extraordinarily wide-ranging and mature discussion, and it had obtained the greatest possible agreement. If the text of the schema was still unclear, the only thing to do was to clarify its formulation, I thought. But if, as the proponents of the *Nota* maintained, the note contained nothing other than what was found in the conciliar document, then what was the point of composing it and arousing unnecessary tension and conflicting interpretations? The *Nota* was neither discussed nor voted upon, nor did the pope himself subscribe to it. Thus it remained outside of the Council's decisions properly so-called.

Was the distribution of the note in the hall intended, perhaps, to make sure that it would be included in the official record of the Council? On this theory, many thought that the note was not simply a working document of the Theological Commission. Just a few others thought it should have become an obligatory interpretive norm for the chapter in question. On November 15 Dossetti, out of a sense of deep concern, sent a letter to Fr. Carlo Colombo, theological consultant to Paul VI:

Dear Monsignore,
We read the *Relatio* and the *Nota praevia* with an indescribable sense of anguish. I know that some of those who are most familiar with

how things work in Rome, even some who live and work in Rome, were still unable to console themselves as of yesterday evening . . .

Dear Don Carlo, in the name of our long friendship I plead with you not to commit the error that the Holy Father's advisers committed a few days ago in regard to the schema on the missions, that of believing that the present state of distress applies only to some isolated individuals or a minority. Even if—under the pressure of events and almost out of fear of the worst—most have adapted to a lesser evil, there is no doubt that there remains in many a negative and disheartening impression . . .

In the face of the worst that was feared just recently, for some, including myself, the first impression was that not everything had been planned in advance. But further reflection now leads to a more severe assessment. This morning I heard of more than one plan to resist and find ways of opposition particularly if there is an effort to assign any special value to the *Nota praevia*.

But the real problem is not so much that of the note as it is that of the substance of the text and of the *expeditio modorum* [the examination of the amendments], from which even the most reasonable suggestions from the majority have been excluded, leaving only the equivocal and even incorrect amendments. The result is a document without the power of truth, without religious meaning, and without any constructive value. Apart from any question of merit, everyone will feel that the result has been purely tactical and worldly, and that it is not by these avenues that the Church succeeds in explaining its own nature clearly to the world.

I am already thinking about making the greatest effort possible to produce a scholarly assessment and interpretation of the document. No one should be upset if many individuals protest the coarseness of the document and its contradictions, which were truly superfluous anyway, because they were not at all necessary for bringing about a greater guarantee of papal primacy. All of it worked together, instead, for the efficient and deliberate realization of unwelcome consequences.

There naturally remains the problem of the procedure used during those days, and this wound will not be healed easily.

I believe that you—because of the part that you played—must inform the Holy Father the real sentiments of many of us. We are quick to recognize that the pope must have, on occasions such as this, every possibility of making his thoughts known, but we will never acknowledge that the avenue taken in this case was the most honest and responsible one possible, nor that it was persuasive or capable of guaranteeing the prerogatives and prestige of the Supreme Authority.

You [Fr. Colombo] may gauge as you see fit the importance of this letter, which I do not intend to be confidential. I write these things because I feel the need to do so in order to fulfill my meager but binding responsibility. I would not hesitate to repeat the same things to the Holy Father in person, with no interior spite and with the greatest filial respect, but with religious candor.[5]

If the appearance of the note had created emotional turmoil and great irritation, the atmosphere at the assembly became even more tense on November 19, when Cardinal Tisserant, as president of the Council of Presidents and without even consulting the moderators, announced that the Declaration on Religious Freedom could not be submitted to the fathers for the next round of voting. This was because, after the changes that had been made to it, it was really a new document requiring closer examination. Therefore, he said, voting would be postponed until the next phase of the Council.

The announcement was received with great distress, because although it had been made in the name of respect for the rules of order, it seemed to deprive the assembly of its decision-making prerogatives. In fact, Tisserant's announcement should be considered together with the request from a group of Spanish bishops opposed to the Declaration on Religious Freedom, who had decided in a meeting to ask for the rigid application of the rules of order with the intention of delaying the vote. This request had been communicated to the assembly the previous day, accompanied by the announcement that the next day, November 19, the assembly would vote on whether to grant the request or not.

So it seemed to be a serious matter that the Council of Presidents—a body that was usually not very active—would not only decide not to proceed with the vote that had been announced, but also take upon itself the sole responsibility for delaying a document that had been the object of particularly lively anticipation. Not even a letter to the pope signed by 441 of the fathers was able to bring about the vote. The matter seemed even more serious when it became known that since October 24, after the tensions of the previous month, the commission had stopped the drafting of a new version of this text to be presented at the Council.

As if all this were not enough, on November 19 the fathers were also informed that approximately twenty modifications had been introduced to the schema on ecumenism "by way of authority." Because the last voting session was at hand, this meant that the assembly had to reject the entire schema or accept the modifications without discussing them. The changes had been sent by Paul VI, who was even thinking at the time of the possibility of preventing the ratification of the decree. His modifications tended to diminish the impact of the document, reducing its ecumenical significance, which inevitably disappointed many of the bishops, but even more the observers. A few days later Bishop Willebrands, who was the head of the Secretariat for Christian Unity at the time, produced a dramatic reconstruction of this crucial moment. In a certain sense it was a good thing that the conclusion of the work was scheduled for November 21, as this made it impossible for the fathers, many of whom were frustrated and disappointed by these repeated crises, to give vent to their more lively reactions.

The general tension and dissatisfaction that are inevitable in a very large group working closely together increased during the third week of November. The difficulties seemed serious enough to run the Council aground, as had already happened the year before during the second half of October. According to Bishop Zaspe of Argentina, "a general sense of dissatisfaction spread throughout the hall . . . because the Council of Presidents did not permit a vote on the schema *De Libertate Religiosa*. A general climate of annoyance asserted itself. Signatures were gathered for protests to be lodged with the pope."[6] Even though the sense of responsibility felt by the majority of the fathers made it possible to get through the crisis, the Black Week left a considerable wake behind it. It had revealed some of the vulnerabilities of the majority. Furthermore, the effort to reach consensus at all costs, in obedience to an urgent request from the pope, clearly prevailed over the need to make more courageous decisions, decisions more in keeping with the general doctrinal outlook of the Council.

Luis Antonio G. Tagle, in the conclusions to his chapter in our exhaustive study of the Council, observed that "without the Black Week, Vatican II would not have been what, in fact, it was: from it came wonderful lessons, exquisite documents, and breathtaking prospects, but it brought painful wounds as well. The forces put into motion by Vatican II were so powerful that the events of the Black Week were not capable of stopping them. And the Black Week itself is one of those springs that have made Vatican II a font of grace for the Church and the world."[7]

The Church Is in the World

On October 14 the Council was asked to discuss a new project on the life and activity of priests; the schema was judged completely unsatisfying and was sent back to the commission for a radical overhaul. Thus it was possible to bring back the schema on the Eastern Churches, the consideration of which was dominated to a great extent by an effort to coordinate this with the document on ecumenism, which the Secretariat for Christian Unity had developed with a completely different approach. The assessments of the fathers were not one-sided; some of them emphasized that the most significant formulations were already contained in the document on ecumenism, in relation to which the schema in question was decisively out of step. Others were afraid that an ad hoc decree on the Eastern Churches would end up by presenting them simply as appendages to the Latin Church, emphasizing a uniqueness that risked becoming a sense of their inferiority. It appeared that the ancient Eastern rites were being protected as an oddity in a completely Latin world, and not as authentic expressions of the variety within the one Church.

Some thought that this document could be ignored completely, because the new collegial perspective brought back into general awareness the principle of communion among the local Churches, recognizing their primary role in the concrete realization of the one true Church of Christ. Many others were disturbed by this detailed consideration of the problems of the Eastern Churches, given that the Orthodox bishops (Greek, Russian, Middle Eastern, and so on) were not participating members of the Council, and therefore any decision, no matter how enlightened it might be, would inevitably have the effect of fostering division rather than reconciliation. In the end, the document was returned to the commission with instructions to revise it for the final session of that phase of the Council.

By this time all of the anticipation at the Council was directed toward the schema XIII, an extensive project that had passed through many intensive revisions and which, according to widespread hopes, was supposed to be the first "proving ground" of the Church's capacity to enter into dialogue with the world. It is very difficult to understand today the scope of the expectations surrounding this schema at the time; it was spoken of as the masterpiece of the Council, its definitive achievement. Many truly thought that the moment had arrived for the Church, already having defined itself, to devote itself to the problems of the world with clarity and generosity, precisely to the extent to which it was sure of being distinct from the world while still sharing responsibility for its salvation.

But what was lacking was the spiritual and doctrinal preparation necessary for proceeding on solid theological foundations. It was easier to request that the Church leave behind its mistrustful and combative attitude toward modernity than that it devise an attitude of friendship without becoming slavish. The momentum generated by John XXIII's encyclical *Pacem in Terris* indicated the possibility, and the benefits, of overcoming the boundaries created by ideological opposition. The great movements of human progress deserved good will and cooperation.

The discussion finally came to the assembly on October 20. During the preparatory phase, before it was presented to the fathers, the document already had undergone a complex series of revisions, a clear symptom of the difficulty of setting into motion an issue that had been dominated for too long by an attitude toward modern society and culture that saw the Church simultaneously in the extreme roles of victor and victim. One working group had followed another, each giving rise to its own project. Thus there was a "Roman" version; a version "of Malines," composed in French by Belgian and French authors, and finally a "Zurich" version, produced in that city in February 1964.[8] The project extended over four chapters dedicated to the theological foundations of the Church's service to the world, to poverty, to overpopulation, and to war. These were the main realities afflicting humanity. The text was presented during a general congregation by Italy's Bishop Guano, and after a brief discussion it received a majority vote in favor (1,576 in favor, 296 against), which permitted further discussion of the various chapters.

The tone of the discussion was serious and purposeful, as was fitting for the topic. One of the needs most frequently mentioned was that for a more extensive and thorough biblical foundation for the presence of the Church in the world and for its relationships with different social groups. According to many of the fathers, the schema lacked a clear basic theological orientation and did not strike a balance between the importance of the renewal of creation through the incarnation and the irreplaceable role of the cross of Christ as characteristic of the Christian presence. Still lacking was sufficient theological reflection to make it possible to reach fully satisfying formulations.

The most perceptive theologians made significant efforts to dampen expectations in regard to this theme. Ratzinger, for example, maintained that "one must not expect very much from this schema, which can be nothing other than the beginning of a discussion that must be carried out over the following decades." If schema XIII was one of the ways in which the Church addressed the problems in the world, it was not the only way, and perhaps not even the most important. A number of the fathers thought of it as a gesture of good will more than anything else.

Surely the most effective contribution the Council could make to an authentic dialogue between the Church and the world was the Church's consistent implementation of its own renewal, which had already been begun, however timidly. A Church more free from worldly concerns, which had rediscovered its own profound nature as the people of God on pilgrimage through history, gathered around the word and the Eucharist, would be so new and so dynamic that it would make a decisive contribution to the progress of humanity. The experience of John XXIII was eloquent in this regard. His miracle had been that of making the sincerity of his message truly believable for everyone.

But there were not many who expressed the problem in such explicit terms. This was partly because it is difficult to make the rhythms of theological reflection coincide with immediate deadlines. This reflection requires long periods of time, and it requires, above all, a favorable, stimulating spiritual and cultural climate. As is now clear, it was this climate that had been lacking for too long, and it could not be replaced by the undeniable good will of the bishops and theologians of the Council. Besides, the optimism that was widespread in the West during those years threatened to taint the work of the Council in this regard.

In any case, the fathers learned that Paul VI had decided on a fourth period of work to be held in 1965, after the November 21 conclusion of the phase in progress. Meanwhile, as they were discussing the schema on relations between the Church and the world, it became evident that the European and Western bias of this project diminished its universal impact and created dissatisfaction among the bishops of other continents. It also emerged that the attitudes of some groups of bishops toward crucial topics were seriously conditioned by the social and political environment of their countries of origin. This was the case, for example, with the topic of peace for the bishops of the United States. There was, therefore, a risk that the central aim of the schema—the active engagement of Christians in the world toward solutions for the dramatic problems of hunger, racism, the arms race, and peace—was prejudiced by the fact that Churches as well as individuals were involved in, or even compromised by, the existing situation and their exercise of cultural, financial, or political power.

From this point of view the Council's attitude toward war and nuclear deterrence was crucial. During those years the arms race was the ruling concern in relations between the two opposing political-military blocs (Western and Soviet). While John XXIII had proclaimed in *Pacem in Terris* that the idea of "just war" had become obsolete in terms of both history and theology, a more timid attitude prevailed in the discussions of the Council. These took up the old distinction between just and unjust war, and accepted, although as a lesser evil, the existence of nuclear arsenals and the manufacturers that supplied them. Any voice on the opposite side would have remained isolated in the face of the stubbornness of the United States bishops, who could count on the understanding of the pope.

It was precisely in order to overcome difficulties such as this that some fathers tried to insist upon the need for the Council to promote the Church's liberation from historical conditioning that obscured its evangelical clarity. It was from this perspective that Cardinal Lercaro proposed the Church's need for cultural poverty, obviously not in the sense of ignorance, but rather as a renunciation of the covetous possession of a finished and closed conceptual system. The Church would, instead, place itself in a posture of openness toward all cultures as equally capable of receiving the gospel message and widening the horizons of the faith. The Church would need to accept being poor and renouncing a proclamation of the gospel wrapped up in a single cultural formulation, which was not essential to the message itself, but indeed sometimes the cause of incomprehension, as had happened on many occasions.

On October 10, 1963, Paul VI had asked Lercaro to examine the material produced by the Church of the Poor Group, with a view toward using it in conciliar documents. In September 1964, at the renewed insistence of the pope, Lercaro devoted himself more intensely to this work in order to comply with the request of the previous year. On November 19 he made a report that began by mentioning the lack of preparation among Catholics on the question of poverty, and thus the provisional nature of the proposals made. This was followed by two sections, one doctrinal and the other practical. The first asserted that an opulent society, far from promoting the general welfare of humanity and overcoming poverty, aggravates the imbalances among classes and peoples and obscures the sense of the sacred, leading to the worship of material goods and a result worse than that of Marxist atheism. The Christian conception of the mystery of poverty needed to be elaborated in both its biblical and christological dimensions.

The second part suggested the gradual introduction of concrete reforms. First, the bishops were to be invited to greater simplicity and evangelical poverty—in regard to their titles, clothing, and way of life—and to select, form, and support priests—or even true worker-priests—as part of an apostolate for the poor and the working classes. Then all Christians would be encouraged to engage in appropriate initiatives, such as giving offerings for the poor and the needy instead of the usual practice of fasting and abstinence. After the conclusion of the Council, these "demonstrations of good will" were to be extended and translated into Church structures and laws. Among these would be a greater participation of the laity in the administration of Church assets and a gradual opening to the public of the Church's financial accounts. The report was sent "for due examination" to Cardinal Tisserant, president of the Commission for the Revision of Clerical Dress and Adornment and . . . went absolutely nowhere.

From November 4 to 6, while the first discussion on schema XIII was being concluded, the assembly again received the document on the bishops and the governance of dioceses, corrected by the commission but still the object of an elevated number of amendments—almost a thousand for each of the first two chapters—which would not permit its definitive approval in the solemn session scheduled for November 21. November 6 also brought the introduction of the project on missionary activity. This was the third topic—and this time it was completely new—that the Council had been called to face in the span of just a few days, while the approach of the conclusion of this third phase brought a need for documents ready for definitive approval.

In this environment the document on the missionary activity of the Church was thrown out after three days. It came from a completely insufficient perspective in terms of the state of missionary awareness that had been emerging during those years under the influence of the sweeping process of decolonization and the participation at the Council of bishops from mission countries. After the painful failure of an ill-advised appeal on the part of the pope to have the Council accept the schema as a basis for discussion, on November 9 the commission itself proposed the withdrawal of the document for further elaboration.

The failure of the schema on missionary activity cleared the way for the presentation of the project on the renewal of religious life, which was presented to the assembly on November 10 and then discussed only until November 12, when it was sent back to the commission. Analogously, from November 17 to 19 the Council discussed the project on Christian education, and especially Catholic schools, which like the preceding document was judged abstract and lackluster. It appeared that the assembly was dominated by pressure from minorities such as the bishops belonging to religious orders or those involved in managing Catholic schools.

Better success was obtained during those same days by the proposals for priestly formation, especially because they provided for significant responsibility on the part of the episcopal conferences in the determination of the course of studies for seminarians. The assembly was bogged down in a jumble of disparate topics and unsatisfying schemata, giving the impression of simply seeking to fulfill its formal requirements. The idea seemed to be that the projects that had been begun in the 1961–62 period and then survived the pruning of 1962–63 should meet their deadlines, no matter what.

The last two general congregations (November 19 and 20, 1964) were occupied by a brief—but elevated and humane—discussion of a document on the sacrament of matrimony, which dealt with impediments to matrimony, mixed marriages, the question of consent, and the form of the celebration of the sacrament. The bond of love uniting the spouses seemed to take on a real dimension for the first time in an ecclesiastical context: many of the fathers made an effort to transcend the usual Scholastic distinctions of the three ends of marriage and to leave behind cold canonical legalism. They tried instead to present in its entirety this profound act of communion between two persons, the closest form of union possible between two creatures, which Christ used as an analogy to his own relationship with the Church. While avoiding any accommodation to the practice of birth control, out of its pastoral concern the Council also strove to avoid creating barriers between individuals and the Church. It made a serious effort to embrace the reality of marriage as profoundly as possible, given the contemporary state of secular and theological understanding. The discussion ended with an acceptance of the proposal from the moderator, Cardinal Döpfner, to leave this topic for the pope.

November 21, 1964: Lumen Gentium

On November 21, in spite of the deep gloom of recent days, the *Dogmatic Constitution on the Church, Lumen Gentium,* was solemnly approved (with 2,151 votes in favor and 5 opposed). Also approved were the Decree on Ecumenism, *Unitatis Redintegratio* (2,137 in favor, 11 opposed) and the Decree on the Eastern Catholic Churches, *Orientalium Ecclesiarum* (2,110 in favor, 39 opposed). The near unanimity in the voting on both the Constitution on the Church and the Decree on Ecumenism, which perhaps came as a surprise, was a reward for the firmness with which the great majority of the fathers had upheld the renewed ecclesiology contained in the constitution, and also the long and patient work of mediation on the part of Paul VI. But it was undeniable that these were patchwork documents, and only time would tell if this would undermine their doctrinal clarity and historical impact.

The constitution on the Church—the only one apart from that on the word of God to receive the label *dogmatic*—opened with the assertion that

> Christ is the light of humanity; and it is, accordingly, the heart-felt desire of this sacred Council, being gathered together in the Holy Spirit, that, by proclaiming his Gospel to every creature (cf. Mk. 16:15), it may bring to all men the light of Christ which shines out visibly from the Church.
>
> Since the Church, in Christ, is in the nature of sacrament—a sign and instrument, that is, of communion with God and of unity among all men—she here proposes, for the benefit of the faithful and of the whole world, to set forth, as clearly as possible, and in the tradition laid down by earlier Councils, her own nature and universal mission. The condition of the modern world lends greater urgency to this duty of the Church; for, while men of the present day are drawn ever more closely together by social, technical and cultural bonds, it still remains for them to achieve full unity in Christ. (*LG*, 1)

The strong points of the document come in the first three chapters, in which the Council, following the path of patristic tradition and the theological renewal of the first half of the twentieth century, presents the Church as "a sacrament in Christ, light of the nations," the linchpin of the Father's plan of salvation. The goal of this plan is the kingdom of heaven, which is distinct from the Church on pilgrimage through history. According to *Lumen Gentium* (9):

> Christ instituted this new covenant, namely the new covenant in his blood (cf. 1 Cor. 11:25); he called a race made up of Jews and Gentiles which would be one, not according to the flesh, but in the Spirit, and this race would be the new People of God . . . That messianic people has as its head Christ . . .
>
> The state of this people is that of the dignity and freedom of the sons of God, in whose hearts the Holy Spirit dwells as in a temple. Its law is the new commandment to love as Christ loved us (cf. John 13:34). Its destiny is the kingdom of God which has been begun by God himself on earth and which must be further extended until it is brought to perfection by him at the end of time . . . hence that messianic people, although it does not actually include all men, and at times may appear as a small flock, is, however, a most sure seed of unity, hope and salvation for the whole human race.

St. Paul's cherished image of the Church as the "body of Christ" is also used by Vatican II, but in the context of a rich and complex elaboration of the biblical images of the Church, which brings a greater variety of aspects and features: it is a people on a journey toward the fulfillment of salvation.

God has renewed an eternal covenant with this people, a covenant brought to completion through the cross and resurrection of Christ. With Jesus and through the work of the Spirit, all the members of the Church participate through faith in the common priesthood, which they exercise primarily in the sacraments, in reciprocal communion, and in service to humanity according to the charisms that each has received. According to *Lumen Gentium* (10):

> The baptized, by regeneration and the anointing of the Holy Spirit, are consecrated to be a spiritual house and a holy priesthood, that through all the works of Christian men they may offer spiritual sacrifices and proclaim the perfection of him who has called them out of darkness into his marvelous light (cf. 1 Pet. 2:4–10). Therefore all the disciples of Christ, persevering in prayer and praising God (Acts 2:42–47), should present themselves as a sacrifice, living, holy and pleasing to God (cf. Rom. 12:1). They should everywhere on earth bear witness to Christ and give an answer to everyone who asks a reason for the hope of an eternal life which is theirs (cf. 1 Pet. 3:15).

The ecclesial community lives in human society and participates in its affairs, but precisely because it is catholic and missionary, it does not identify itself with any particular social, cultural, or racial condition. The Church of Christ is realized within the Catholic Church, which is headed by the Roman pontiff—the center of the college of bishops—but it is not exhausted by it. The expression in *Lumen Gentium* (8) according to which the true Church subsists—that is, it is realized without being exhausted—in the Roman Catholic Church ignited a frivolous debate. In order to avoid the attribution of the term *Church* to other communities (for example, Orthodox, Protestant, Anglican), some of the conservatives wanted to color the understanding of the Church expressed at the Council on the basis of a contorted interpretation of this single formula taken out of context, with no reference to the whole of the Council's teaching.[9]

According to the Council, by divine will the Church is endowed with ministers whose authority is at the service of their brothers and sisters. As successors to the apostles instituted by Christ himself, the bishops continue this work of service and constitute a body, or college, which is the expression of the communion joining the sister churches over which they preside. By episcopal consecration, the highest degree of the sacrament of holy orders, the college receives new members who, in order to be part of this college legitimately, must be in communion with the Bishop of Rome. So, through their sacramental consecration the bishops participate in Christ's threefold authority to teach, sanctify, and rule. They do so individually for their local Churches, and for the universal Church when they are united together and united with the Bishop of Rome.

The Council asserts:

> In order to fulfill such lofty functions, the apostles were endowed by Christ with a special outpouring of the Holy Spirit coming upon them (cf. Acts 1:8; 2:4; John 20:22–23), and, by the imposition of hands (cf. 1 Timothy 4:14; 2 Timothy 1:6–7), they passed on to their auxiliaries the gift of the Spirit, which is transmitted down to our day through episcopal consecration. The holy synod teaches, moreover, that the fullness of the sacrament of Orders is conferred by episcopal consecration, that fullness, namely, which both in the liturgical tradition of the Church and in the language of the Fathers of the Church is called the high priesthood, the acme of the sacred ministry. Now, episcopal consecration confers, together with the office of sanctifying, the duty also of teaching and ruling, which, however, of their very nature can be exercised only in hierarchical communion with the head and members of the college . . . It is the right of bishops to admit newly elected members into the episcopal body by means of the sacrament of Orders. (*LG*, 21)

Lumen Gentium represented a clear step forward with respect to both the decisions of Vatican Council I and the increased rigidity of the papal magisterium in the decades following it. Contrary to what had been foreseen, the Council fathers were not content simply to place recognition of the rights of the bishops beside the prerogatives of the pope. Not limiting itself to the legal-institutional dimension, the document's great spiritual and theological dynamism brought forth an image of the Church as a mystery, while respecting this living body that is continually growing under the impulse of the Spirit. The distinction made between the kingdom of God and the Church, and between the one Church of Christ and the different ecclesial traditions, overcame the shortsighted complacency from which a large part of anti-reformist theology had suffered during recent centuries. This was an impressive first step toward an escape from the so-called Constantinian era, with its much-deplored triumphalism, and toward a purification from clericalism.

In its turn, the Decree on Ecumenism *(Unitatis Redintegratio)* thankfully brought Catholicism out of its long period of inactivity in regard to the restoration of Christian unity. The document begins by asserting:

> The restoration of unity among all Christians is one of the principal concerns of the Second Vatican Council. Christ the Lord founded one Church and one Church only. However, many Christian communions present themselves to men as the true inheritors of Jesus Christ; all indeed profess to be followers of the Lord but they differ in mind and go their different ways, as if Christ himself were divided. Certainly, such division openly contradicts the will of Christ,

scandalizes the world, and damages that most holy cause, the preaching of the Gospel to every creature. (*UR*, 1)

In the spirit of this assertion the Council recognized the necessity of overcoming the mutual opposition of the various doctrinal systems. It accepted the principle that different ways and methods of proclaiming the faith could complement one another, and that the truths of Christian doctrine occupy different positions in the hierarchy of revelation:

> The manner and order in which Catholic belief is expressed should in no way become an obstacle to dialogue with our brethren . . . In ecumenical dialogue, Catholic theologians, standing fast by the teaching of the Church yet searching together with separated brethren into the divine mysteries, should do so with love for the truth, with charity, and with humility. When comparing doctrines with one another, they should remember that in Catholic doctrine there exists an order or "hierarchy" of truths, since they vary in their relation to the foundation of the Christian faith. (*UR*, 11)

The old outlook according to which unity would be realized through the "return" of the "heretics" and "schismatics" to the Roman Church was finally left behind. It was particularly significant that a model of unity had been created, not on the basis of uniformity and absorption, but on the variety of charisms and the complementarity of the different traditions. The Council even asserted that

> every renewal of the Church essentially consists in an increase of fidelity to her own calling . . . Christ summons the Church, as she goes her pilgrim way, to that continual reformation of which she always has need, insofar as she is an institution of men here on earth. Consequently, if, in various times and circumstances, there have been deficiencies in moral conduct or in Church discipline, or even in the way the Church's teaching has been formulated—to be carefully distinguished from the deposit of faith itself—these should be set right at the opportune moment and in the proper way. (*UR*, 6)

Finally, the brief decree on the Eastern Catholic Churches (*Orientalium Ecclesiarum*), which had survived the repeated perplexities expressed in its regard (in part by the relatively high number of opposing votes in the solemn sessions), considered the particular value of the Eastern Churches in union with Rome (for example, Coptic, Chaldean, Armenian, Maronite, Melkite, Ukrainian). These were recognized as local Churches endowed with their own legitimate variety in terms of liturgy (rites and languages), institutions (patriarchates, synods, the selection of bishops), and discipline (clerical celibacy).

The atmosphere in the assembly had changed. The Council had grown in terms of the awareness of the bishops, who were fulfilling their duty of guiding the universal Church with greater courage and clarity. It had also grown in the sense that, from a focus on Western Europe, it had passed to a sense of commitment and initiative involving almost all the different groups of bishops, from the Africans to the Latin Americans, thus attaining a real universality. Still, there were serious questions about the increased number of interventions by the pope during the last week. The last of these had been the pope's surprising proclamation, during the concluding session, of Mary as Mother of the Church. The Council had not inserted this title into the text of *De Ecclesia* because it had not seemed, from a theological point of view, clear or well founded.

Did the Council have freedom of action, or was it directed from outside? The absence of a true authority responsible for the direction of the assembly had been displayed on a number of occasions, and not even the moderators had been able to fill this gap, for a number of reasons. This left room for uncertainties and doubts to be exaggerated, for some, beyond their real dimensions. It was also true that the interventions of the pope had not substantially changed anything. But they did have a moderating and limiting effect, which, if anything, had diminished the clarity and vigor of the documents by seeking to make them more nuanced and to place them within a more customary context. These had undeniably been interventions corresponding to the concerns of the minority Council groups, even the most insignificant ones in terms of both quality and number, who had never asked themselves whether the convictions of the majority might be a good for the entire ecclesial community or whether they might represent a powerful movement of the Holy Spirit's action within the Church and thus should be accepted in their original formulations. Or was there, instead, the pope's personal judgment of the Council's expression behind all this, and his decisive preference for a prudent centrism?

Some of the passages from the concluding speech of Paul VI can be understood in this sense. On the whole, the speech was characterized by an attitude of caution toward collegiality and cited the interpretation formulated by the *Nota*. It was a speech that repeatedly made reference to the pope's satisfaction with the insistent and continual reaffirmation of papal primacy in the document. The practical consequences of the recognition of the college of bishops were indicated as consisting in the collaboration in the postconciliar commissions on the part of the episcopal bodies; in the possibility of consulting a certain number of bishops at particular times, a clear reference to the synods of bishops; and in the intention of integrating the departments of the Curia with some of the diocesan bishops. Many had the impression that the tone of the pope's speech had slackened in comparison with his previous speeches, which had been so committed to a Christocentric conception of the Church.

Results and Uncertainties

When the Catholic bishops returned to Rome during the second week of September 1964 for the next phase of the Council's work, the situation of the world was marked by significant new developments. On the general political level, the situation in Vietnam had worsened following increased military engagement on the part of the United States. The People's Republic of China announced that it had the atomic bomb, breaking the monopoly over atomic weapons previously maintained by Britain, France, the Soviet Union, and the United States. Then, on October 15, 1964, Nikita Khrushchev fell from power in Moscow. Following this came a slowdown in the process of de-Stalinization and a further weakening of the Soviet regime. These events were followed with apprehension and concern, especially by the Asian bishops participating in the Council.

The internal composition of the Council assembly had changed considerably yet again. About 250 of the fathers (a good 10 percent of them) were participating in the Council's work either for the first time during this third period or without having participated in the work of 1963. They brought a fresh contribution that could also have represented a source of discontinuity. In its first decisions Vatican II displayed an interesting and pronounced inversion of tendencies that had prevailed within Catholicism for at least four centuries. This was especially true in regard to the relationship between the Church and history. A negative interpretation of history following the irreversible decline of Christendom saw the Church as a citadel under siege, engaged in a form of trench warfare in which refusal to change seemed the best—if not the only—form of resistance possible. But if Christianity is seen instead as something that is lived out within the contradictions of human history, in which the search for Christ is conducted through human beings and events and not in spite of them, then the Church's authentic nature is shown to be that of a communion with Christ and among human beings on a journey in which everything is called to change, apart from the gospel.

The perspective of the Church as being on a journey, which the Council proposed, was perhaps more a sketch of basic schemata than a completed and integral design. Some of the bishops and theologians made an effort to emphasize the role of the Holy Spirit in the dynamic of the Church, all the more so in consideration of the importance accorded to the Holy Spirit in the Eastern Christian tradition. But this effort did not succeed in overcoming the excessive tendency to refer to Christ and the marginal role accorded to the Holy Spirit seen in the overall structure of the Council's declarations. The effects of this were particularly severe in regard to the relationship between the Church and history. In this case it was not enough simply to evoke the role of the Spirit; instead, the expression of this role needed to be deepened and elaborated.

Lumen Gentium also recovered the importance of the universal priest-hood of the faithful, and, after a long overshadowing fraught with conse-quences, reopened (in no. 12) the possibility of taking into account the "sense of the faithful" *(sensus fidelium)*, which traditionally expresses itself in the consensus of the community of the faithful and its acceptance, or lack of acceptance, of the teachings of the magisterium.

A great number of the bishops, especially the ones from Italy and Spain, had a hard time coming to terms with religious freedom as something other than the freedom of the Church itself. The phrase had been a glori-ous emblem of many battles that had taken place over the centuries [as the Church struggled with kings, queens, princes, and emperors for its free-dom]. The Pauline theme of the individual Christian's freedom, which had been forcefully reintroduced by Martin Luther, had been brought up in the discussions only timidly—and to the discomfort of many. Too few of the Council fathers were able to understand intuitively the importance that this theme would have in the context of the increasingly widespread religious pluralism in Western society.

Even more than this, it was perhaps harder for the bishops to overcome the insidious anti-Semitism implicit on so many levels of the Catholic spirit and to acknowledge the theological importance—as mysterious as this might be—of the Jewish people. It may be true that the tortuous paths of the Declaration on Religious Freedom and the Declaration on the Jews dem-onstrated political influences—as the Vatican Secretary of State in fact maintained—but it would be hypocritical to ignore the profound causes of these difficulties. They were rooted in an inveterate Christian, and par-ticularly Catholic, hostility toward the principle of democracy and the "per-fidious Jews," a hostility that began to be reversed only with John XXIII. After the heavy-handed teaching of Pius XII, who had suggested drawing the criteria for social organization directly from revelation, the manifesta-tions of genuine openness to the problems of modern society had come from two encyclicals by John XXIII: *Mater et Magistra* and *Pacem in Terris*. It must be emphasized that the impact of these new developments and the acceleration of changes in the world had also had important effects on the internal equilibrium of the Council assembly. These are, in fact, the issues that impelled the Council to try to move beyond the exclusive focus on Greco-Latin culture and Roman-Germanic law that had marked Catholi-cism since late antiquity. For their part, the English-speaking bishops found in this an opportunity to move beyond their longstanding cultural and civic marginalization, which had been evident in the development of Ca-tholicism in North America during the 1970s. For the bishops of the Third World, the atmosphere of inquiry and understanding toward the great monotheistic religions brought the possibility for a less subservient form of participation in the Council's work.

Every Tuesday afternoon during this third period the observers at the Council and representatives of the Secretariat for Christian Unity had continued to hold productive meetings on topics under discussion in the assembly. The reports that the observers frequently sent to their churches, even during the recess, were a further testimony of their intense participation at Vatican II, even though the observers coming from the Orthodox world sometimes experienced considerable difficulty in getting their bearings. As he had in 1962, Paul VI continued to maintain that the aim of Vatican II was the determination of teaching about the Church, and especially about the bishop's office, in "connection with Vatican Council I," of which Vatican II was "the logical continuation." He continued to stress this interpretation in spite of the fact that Pope John XXIII had explicitly excluded it. Paul VI, in his ceaseless effort to obtain the greatest unanimity possible at the Council—by means of a particularly close relationship with Felici, in addition to Cardinal Cicognani, the Secretary of State—had brought himself closer to the Curia, thereby avoiding the considerable risk that the Curia might establish direct ties with the Council minority, creating deep divisions among the bishops. Within the daily relations between the pope and the Council, increasing importance was accorded to the petitions made by the bishops to Paul VI. These then gave rise to the frequent interventions on the part of pope during the composition of the documents—at the level of the commissions or subcommissions rather than during the discussions in the Council. This avoided the violent trauma caused by untimely interventions during the discussions themselves (for example, the one resulting in the preliminary explanatory note for the amendments to chapter III of *De Ecclesia*, or the difficulties surrounding the schema on ecumenism). But this implied, almost by necessity, modes of participation that were extremely discreet, or even secretive, in contradiction to the transparency required for the Council's unhindered operation.

The events of these weeks clearly showed the majority's determination to carry the work forward according to its own deeply held convictions. But they also displayed the weaknesses of the process, its patchwork nature, and its essentially European and North American cultural composition. The Council as a whole, the Council majority, and the directive bodies coordinated by the majority gradually lost cohesion and efficiency. The sense that the body of bishops was the real main character of the Council, a sense that had been widespread during the first two periods, began to lose its intoxicating effect. What came to replace it, in addition to a greater sense of uneasiness, was a certain sense of fatigue. This was certainly understandable after fifty or so general congregations, in addition to countless sessions, meetings, and encounters, in which the most disparate topics had been considered, many of them distasteful to the great majority of the Council fathers.

It seemed that, faced with the challenge of promoting the presence of the Christian faith and the Church in history—without protection or privileges—Vatican II was suffering from a case of dizziness. The whole

Council watched in Rome as a more and more bitter debate raged between the first postconciliar body, the Council for the Implementation of the Liturgical Commission (headed by one of the moderators, Giacomo Lercaro) and the Curial Congregation for Rites. One got the impression that the offices of the Curia were unwilling to hand over their responsibility for ensuring fidelity to the Council's decrees to entities that had not existed before Vatican II. More generally, was this perhaps an attempt by groups within the Roman Curia to deprive the conclusions of the Council of any real meaning? A week before the approval of *Lumen Gentium*, on November 14, 1964, Cardinal Ruffini, Archbishop of Palermo, had suggested in a letter to Paul VI that he reserve a reasonable period of time after the end of the Council's work for revising and finalizing the documents before promulgating them during a solemn concluding ceremony.

It is undeniable that this third phase of the Council was tempestuous and combative, and that its atmosphere was less lofty than that of the two preceding periods. But one must not underestimate the importance of the progress that was made. The huge mechanism of Vatican II continued to function as a living body, with both consistencies and surprises with respect to its own past. The chief result of this third period of work seems to have been that of bringing to completion the work begun in the first two periods and of successfully navigating the passage to the problems of the Church's relations with the world. It was the proper fulfillment of the duty that the bishops had assumed with their message to humanity on October 20, 1962.

5

The Faith Lives within History
(1965)

The Recess before the Forth Session (1964–1965)

The months between the third and fourth periods (December 1964 to September 1965) were characterized by intensive labor on the part of the Council commissions, which were frequently broken down into a number of subcommissions. These were engaged in the elaboration of a number of new documents, such as that on the missions, or in the complete restructuring of existing documents, such as schema XIII and the schemata on the condition of the priesthood and on religious life.

A special event was held in Rome for reflection on the pontificate of John XXIII, which naturally included reflection on the Council, background for which is recorded over several days in Angelina Nicora's diary:

> Father Giuseppe [Dossetti] is having dinner and staying overnight with us. He has prepared the speech on Pope John that the cardinal [Lercaro] will deliver in Rome. In its essence, it is a bitter and harsh speech and gives a great deal of room to comparisons unfavorable toward the current pontiff. The cardinal would like to moderate the speech in a number of ways: he is especially perplexed by a proposal at the end for the canonization of the pope at the Council. He has discovered that P. [Paul VI] is not happy with this idea, to his own considerable personal embarrassment. The upshot is that the speech will be delivered almost in its entirety [on February 23], except for the final passage about canonization.

> Pippo [Dossetti] himself is convinced that by closing off an emotional outlet the removal of the final section on canonization has made the speech stronger as a whole.

> Bea was present for the speech, and this is very important. It is puzzling why none of the other progressive cardinals attended.[1]

At a public conference on February 23 at the Luigi Sturzo Institute in Rome, Cardinal Lercaro delivered a lecture entitled "Guidelines for the Study of John XXIII," in which he addressed the need for a deeper understanding of the personality of Pope John and for critical reflection on the historical importance of his pontificate and the relationship between his perspectives and the substance of the Council's work. The lecture, which was filled with a sense of conviction about the extraordinary impulse aroused in contemporary Christianity by the Holy Spirit, working through John XXIII, was originally to have concluded with the proposal to have John's canonization deliberated at the Council, according to ancient custom. This would have been

> the necessary crowning moment of all the decisions already made within an ecclesial and historical context in which the person and teaching of Pope John appear to be, in the end, not only the point of departure for Vatican II, but in a certain sense the very object of the Council. In such a case, the proclamation of the holiness of John XXIII would constitute the definitive approval of the Council's decisions and the necessary guarantee of their effective reception into the life of the Church. But this does not mean a simple recognition of his exemplary holiness, such as that of other saints. It means acknowledging his holiness as a creative force in the introduction of a new era for the Church, and the identification of this holy pastor, doctor, and prophet as an anticipation of this new era.

Lercaro, however, decided to omit this conclusion,[2] partly because Paul VI didn't like the idea of a conciliar canonization. In the lecture he maintained that

> the Council was not only the greatest, most demanding, and most consequential decision that the pope made during his lifetime, but it was and would continue to be the great sustaining force, the enduring dynamo of his plan for his pontificate. But this appeal to the Council and the Council majority, which is substantially in agreement with the main points of John's vision, especially in regard to Christian optimism, the essential religious nature of the Church, the need for a thawing of ideological opposition, ecumenism, service on behalf of peace in the world, and so forth, cannot be an appeal to something automatic. It cannot be an appeal to what some like to refer to as irreversible, which operates almost magically apart from certain historical conditions characterized by a persevering effort of fidelity.

He added:

I would not be so sure that everything that Pope John actually expected from the Council, and in general hoped would be the historical and religious achievement of our generation, has already been realized, or even nearly so. It is not even clear that a gradual process of implementation has begun that excludes the possibility of regression, interruption, or partial undoing.

This was a courageous way of explicitly presenting the disturbing but real question of Vatican II's consistency with itself and, above all, with the character that Pope John had wished to impart to it.

Sunday, March 7, 1965, had seen the inauguration of the celebration of the Mass according to the updated rite, with much of the ceremony in the native language and with the altar turned toward the people. Paul VI himself had celebrated the Mass in Italian in a Roman parish on that day and had exhorted the parish priests to collaborate in the implementation of the reform. This liturgical renewal was probably the main area in which all the faithful, even the most humble, could gauge the significance of the reforms introduced by the Council. It is difficult to overstate the importance of this. The range of reactions to the liturgical reform and to the other aspects of the conciliar renewal displayed during the spring and summer of 1965 are particularly interesting because they bring to light the characteristics and the difficulties of the first phases of the Council's reception. From the announcements made by the bishops and the episcopal conferences, one can gather that conservatives were the first to express concern.

April 9, 1965, brought the announcement of the creation of the Secretariat for Nonbelievers, which was in perfect harmony with the new season inaugurated by Vatican II: it was important to delineate the aims and methods of the new body, which fit so well within the conciliar climate and the expectations created by the discussion of schema XIII and by the Paul VI's encyclical *Ecclesiam Suam*. The newly appointed president of the secretariat, Austrian Cardinal Franz König, said that

> this was not a question of organizing the fight against atheism, even militant atheism, but rather of considering all the possible ways of assuring for religion the place that rightly belongs to it within society, of establishing contacts with the aim of engaging in a dialogue on an intellectual level, of encouraging concerted efforts on behalf of peace.[3]

The secretariat was to establish contact with doctrinal atheism in all of its forms, even when these did not correspond directly to any political power. This permitted moving beyond the perspective of reducing atheism to atheism of the state, that is, to the Soviet world. It was no secret that there would be difficulties in this task, partly because, first of all, the possible partners of such a dialogue had to be identified.

Care was taken to avoid the interpretation that the secretariat would have a political and diplomatic role. In fact, with his assumption of the presidency of the secretariat, König would need an additional title in order to continue pursuing reconciliation between Catholicism and the communist countries (Ostpolitik), an initiative begun by John XXIII in which König, as Bishop of Vienna, had been involved for a number of years. The creation of the Secretariat for Nonbelievers was situated within the wider and more complex panorama of initiatives related to determining the relationship between the Catholic Church and the communist world. John XXIII's death and the downfall of Khrushchev had undoubtedly ushered in new scenarios, in which enthusiasm seemed to be replaced by a certain measure of diplomatic reflection, even though it appeared difficult to interrupt a dialogue that had taken so much effort to bring in into being.

There were various points of view on these matters within the Catholic Church; Paul VI had accentuated the necessity of the Church's freedom, not for reasons of prestige, but in order to respect the natural aspiration of human beings and to permit the Church to proclaim the gospel and "offer to the construction of a less unjust world the contribution that it, and only it, can bring." The words of Paul VI reemphasized the superiority of the Catholic Church and seemed to limit dialogue with the communist world to the diplomatic sphere. There was also another part of the ecclesiastical world that had looked on Pope John's initiatives of openness with concern: for them, communism was still the main enemy, and instead of approving formulas favorable to dialogue, they felt the Council should have issued a further condemnation of Marxism.

Proponents of the French and Italian communist parties who were involved in various ways in the dialogue taking place between Marxists and Catholics in the secular sphere emphasized the role of John XXIII's pontificate and Vatican II in opening a new era of relations in which condemnation had given way to dialogue, as shown by the creation of the secretariat. This debate also entered the Council hall. On several occasions attempts had been made to insert a condemnation of communism within schema XIII, but it had always been set aside for reasons of expedience, putting off a definitive decision. As the conclusion of Vatican II approached, the question of defining a relationship with Marxism resurfaced. The fathers were required to choose condemnation, silence, or dialogue. Without a doubt, the creation of the Secretariat for Nonbelievers favored dialogue.

On January 4, 1965, Paul VI set September 14 as the date for the resumption of the general congregation's work. The next phase of the Council promised to be full of excitement. Although public opinion was not informed in detail of the work undertaken in the commissions, many of the topics that these were considering were of great common interest and were widely reported by the press. It was expected that the schema on the bishops would clarify in concrete terms the exercise of episcopal collegiality and the renewal of the bishop's stature and pastoral role.

The lay organizations, which during the spring and summer months had held many internal meetings and discussions, looked with great hope to the schema on the apostolate of the laity. The definition of the "people of God" was waiting to receive concrete realization in the renewal of the position of the faithful in the Church and the redefinition of their relationship with the hierarchy.

The summer of 1964 had also seen the assemblies (general chapters) of various religious orders, including very prominent ones such as the Jesuits and the Dominicans, who were preparing themselves for the renewal that the Council might bring about in the sphere of religious life. Similar expectations accompanied the schema on the life and ministry of priests and the schema on seminaries.

The schema on the Church in the modern world fostered strong interest in ecclesial circles in regard to the new developments that were expected in the definition of the relationship between the Church and temporal realities. As for the question of birth control, a topic followed with great attention by public opinion, it was widely known that Paul VI had nominated an extraconciliar commission to examine this and hope was still alive that the Council might have something new to say in this regard.

The expectations of public opinion were even stronger in regard to the topic of peace. The urgent appeal for a reduction in military spending that Paul VI had made while on a visit to Mumbai in December 1964 had aroused modest interest within diplomatic circles, beyond the requisite expressions of appreciation. The international situation, which was characterized by the agonizing and frequently dramatic processes of decolonization in Africa and Asia, was strongly influenced by the clash among the great world powers for control over the new countries.

There was similarly lively interest in regard to the other schemata: that on religious liberty and the one on Judaism, both of which were full of significance for life in many countries.

On June 12 the General Secretary had sent five of the eleven projects to the fathers for discussion. On the eve of the opening of the next phase of work, the main preoccupations of Paul VI seemed to be with the risks of an overeager reception of the Council's proposed innovations and with the problem of establishing a proper relationship with the modern world and overcoming the rigid separation between the Christian faith and temporal realities. Paul VI had always been open to the realities and needs of the modern world; dialogue with the people of his time, with "the world," was his chief desire. But it is impossible to overlook the change of tone that took place during this period in his references to this reality. It was an indication of the fears that had arisen during those months in the uncertain and tense atmosphere of reactions to the introduction of conciliar innovations into the concrete life of the Church and theological discussion. It was, perhaps, with a less serene and optimistic spirit that Paul VI prepared to open the next phase, in which the problems of the relationship with the modern world would be at the center of everyone's attention.

According to the influential journalist Raniero La Valle:

> The Council is an unknown variable. The Cardinal [Lercaro] believes that the episcopates from outside of Italy are coming back weakened: the Dutch because of their excessive initiatives in regard to the liturgy, the French because of the events surrounding the JEC [Jeunesse Etudiante Chrétienne or Young Christian Students, an organization founded in France]. In the meantime, in a meeting with the Coordinating Commission, Cardinal Cicognani has said that, unlike the members of the Curia, the moderators should not speak, even though the comments of the latter would be an improvement on what is actually said at the Council. I believe that the moderators did not comply with this request, but naturally they found it very disturbing. I remarked [to Cardinal Lercaro] that they should sooner relinquish their position as moderators; they have a greater contribution to make to the universal Church than just giving the fathers permission to speak and stopping them after ten minutes. As for the schemata, although there are still rumors that the document on the Jews will be suppressed, it is still on the order of business. But the Cardinal believes that the condemnation of the charge of deicide will be removed from it again. The passage on marriage and family has disappeared from schema XIII (on the grounds that the pope has reserved the question to himself), and so has the condemnation of nuclear weapons, in a step backward from *Pacem in Terris*. So one will no longer know the Church's stance on peace.
>
> The schema on religious liberty should be good. The first chapter of *De Episcopis* is worrying; until the last moment there is still the possibility that it could be presented as an interpretation of *De Ecclesia* by the same group that approved this document, thus bypassing all of the formal questions connected with the preliminary note. The religious themselves have prepared the schema on religious, so that will just be however it is. My God, what title will I have to come up with for the next book on the Council?
>
> But maybe that problem will not even arise.
>
> Sorry to have gone on so long. I embrace you and your children. Take courage,
>
> Raniero+

Concerns about the period after the Council would certainly influence the developments of the final phase. The experience of the *Consilium* with the application of liturgical reform had shown the importance of how the

Council's decrees were implemented and the need for proceeding with caution. It is no accident that the Secretariat for Christian Unity had tried to lay claim to the creation of guidelines on ecumenism. Entities for the implementation of the Council's decrees were also foreseen in other matters, from the apostolate of the laity to involvement in international organizations, and it was clear that the effectiveness of what had been achieved in the Council would depend upon these groups.

Is There Such a Thing as Religious Liberty?

By this time the aim of the Council was to speak in "the most serene and fraternal harmony" possible, as Paul VI put it, on all of the matters still under discussion. But because of complicated organizational problems, the fourth phase would be characterized more by work in the commissions and voting in the assembly than by the plenary discussions that wore away at the bishops, most of whom were not members of any commission. Most of the fathers wavered between their impatience to bring their long and expensive stay in Rome to an end, and their conviction that the Council could not be concluded without approving the documents on religious liberty and on the condition of the Church in contemporary society.

Everything would take place according to schedule, but at the price of giving up the possibility for deeper elaboration and for the stabilization of the internal dynamic of the assembly. This would create particularly difficult problems for the commissions, which were required to consider a great number of frequently contradictory amendments and thus to compose theologically weak compromise documents.

The opening speech of Paul VI, on September 14, 1965, was received favorably as an act of trust in the Council, which had placed the pastors of the Church "in a state of tension, of spiritual struggle," removing them from the stagnation of everyday life and immersing them in an event of great significance and intense communion. The pope, who on the preceding June 24 had embarked upon the task of the reform of the Roman Curia, the revision of the Code of Canon Law, and the exploration of the question of birth control, surprised the fathers with two other important announcements: the decision to go to the United Nations to plead for peace, and the institution of the synod of bishops. On the eve of the Council's conclusion, the pope was preparing to resume full personal initiative.

The assembly went back to work on September 15, taking up the Declaration on Religious Freedom. The presenter, Bishop De Smedt of Belgium, emphasized that the document did not in any way equate truth with error, nor did it exempt anyone from the duty to seek the truth. The most relevant contributions came from Poland's Cardinal Wyszynski and Cardinal Beran of Czechoslovakia, who had suffered from the denial of freedom first by the Nazis and then under the communist regime. They not only upheld the Church's rights against its persecutors, but they also confessed the errors that had been committed in the name of the Church.

Beran, in particular, evoked the burning at the stake of the Bohemian reformer Hus and the confessionalistic practice of the Hapsburgs, who had made Catholicism the obligatory state religion and a supporter of the throne, according to the principle that the religion of the subjects must be that of their sovereign. He emphasized that violence used on behalf of the faith injures and humiliates the faith itself most of all. This brought to the forefront the duty of condemning violence and of cooperative action in the domain of religious thought, of whatever origin and form. It became increasingly evident that this meant affirming the value of religious freedom for social and political coexistence, which would not prevent the Catholic Church from continuing to consider itself the authentic realization of the true religion. These further considerations even brought many of the Italian bishops, with Cardinal Urbani, Patriarch of Venice, as their spokesman, to vote in favor of the declaration. By November 19 the opposing votes had been reduced to 249.

After the voting on religious liberty, which had taken place only at the level of consultation, from September 23 to 27 the assembly then expressed its judgment on the amended text of the schema on revelation, as well as the project—which had also been amended, partly by Paul VI—on the apostolate of the laity. But by then the Council's attention had focused on the new version of schema XIII, which had been produced by the combined effort of seven different working groups. It was presented on September 21 by Archbishop Garrone of France and approved by the Coordinating Commission in spite of the fact that it was constructed as a sociological treatise rather than a conciliar decree. Discussions on this document would continue until October 6. Criticisms were still numerous and deep. Many rejected the identification of scientific and technological progress with the realization of redemption, which seemed to underlie many passages of the document. There were also problems with the form of expression: the Church wanted to speak to people in a new way, and not in the usual manner of authority and condemnation, and yet it could not place itself on a merely human level. The schema lavishly combined the language of theology and faith with that of the world, ceding too much room—according to some—to philosophical arguments and phenomenological observations.

Some groups at the Council were becoming increasingly aware that it was not possible to improvise over the course of a few months a reflection that had been omitted for centuries or reduced within the narrow categories of the "social doctrine of the Church." What emerged was an unbridgeable gap between the spirit driving the fathers to formulate a new ecclesial attitude toward the world and the completely insufficient conceptual development of the issue. As French Dominican Fr. Chenu, one of the guiding lights of the schema, observed, it was necessary to begin from the conviction that great events of history and great social changes have some bearing on the realization of the kingdom of God, and to learn to recognize the signs of the times as theological sources. This, of course, was the new direction of reflection indicated by *Pacem in Terris*.

The topics most frequently discussed were again those of the family and peace. Bishop Zoghby, a Melkite from Lebanon, created a great ruckus with his presentation of the problem of a spouse abandoned through no fault of his or her own, yet unable to remarry. Without compromising the law of the indissolubility of marriage, he struck an intensely pastoral tone to ask the Church, as a mother, to find a solution that would permit these unhappy children of hers to live in peace as well. In regard to the problem of procreation, which had been turned over to Paul VI, the document would include a series of references to Pius XI's encyclical *Casti Connubi* and Pius XII's speech to obstetricians, emphasizing the Church's constant and unchangeable teaching, even though these documents carried a different authority and were of a lower ranking with respect to a conciliar decision.

Strong declarations would be made on the topic of peace by Cardinals Alfrink (of Holland), Liénart (of France), and Léger (of Canada), who sought to bring the discussion back into the atmosphere and context of the gospel, removing it from the technological and military considerations ("dirty" bombs versus "clean" bombs, the foreseeable number of deaths from an atomic conflict, and so on) that had deadened the debate during the Council's previous phase. War, it was said, had to be condemned because it was contrary to the spirit of the gospel, and not simply because of the terrible consequences that would follow from it, and the condemnation had to be complete, with no exceptions. It is illusory to build peace without condemning any recourse to arms, even for the restoration of violated rights, asserted Archbishop Duval of Algeria, who had certainly had his share of painful experiences in this matter. The final text was weak overall; it retained the admission of defensive war and explicitly condemned only total war. It avoided rejecting the recourse to arms but recognized the moral legitimacy of conscientious objection. As in the case of other topics, the Council was unable to find language in which to express an authentically evangelical position but based itself on positions of the "progressive" groups in the Western world. Formulated in this way there was a risk that the documents would rapidly become out of date. On the other hand, the Council had at last faced the issue: silence was no longer available as a way out.

On October 4, Bishop Bettazzi of Ivrea (Italy), acting as the spokesman of requests that had been circulating for at least a year among the Council fathers, proposed that the Council should solemnly sanction the exemplary holiness of Pope John through a conciliar canonization. This would be both an act of devotion toward the "Pope of the Council" and an act of commitment to following faithfully the lines of development and renewal that he had indicated. The initiative was the resumption of an effort made by Bettazzi himself and some of the groups of bishops from the Third World in 1964, and it echoed the lecture that Lercaro had delivered in Rome the preceding February. But it was blocked by the moderator, Cardinal Suenens, who was aware that Paul VI had some reservations about it. Was there perhaps a fear that such an act on the part of the assembly, which would have reintroduced the ancient practice of conciliar canonizations, would have an uncontrollable, galvanizing effect on the Council?

While the discussion on schema XIII was being concluded, the Council approved *Christus Dominus (Decree on the Pastoral Office of Bishops in the Church)* on bishops and the governance of dioceses, with 2,161 votes in favor. On October 7 it began to examine the document that would become *Ad Gentes (Decree on the Missionary Activity of the Church)*, which had been completely remade. The revision was due mostly to the work of Fr. Johannes Schütte, Superior General of the Society of the Divine Word, who had been assisted by the theologians Congar, Ratzinger, and Seumaois. This theme also brought up the problem of the influence of the conception of the Church that had inspired the *Constitution on the Sacred Liturgy*, the *Dogmatic Constitution on the Church*, and the *Decree on Ecumenism*, which had already received solemn approval.

Among items that came up in the discussion of *Ad Gentes*, one related to the chapter on the people of God in *Lumen Gentium*. Many of the fathers had asked that there be a clarification of how the missionary task is a duty of the *whole* Church. In reality, the project presented missionary activity as

Catholic News Service

Father Joseph Ratzinger, the future Pope Benedict XVI, shown talking here to an unidentified bishop in 1962, was peritus to Cardinal Joseph Frings of Cologne and was an important figure in all four sessions of the Council.

a function of the ecclesiastical hierarchy, which was clearly out of line with the vision of the Church as a communion. The problems from the ecumenical point of view were no less delicate. The great impulse toward Christian union had come from missionary circles, where the competition among Christian missions of different confessions was a glaring scandal. On this point the schema referred to the *Decree on Ecumenism*, asserting that collaboration must take place among Christians on both an individual level and the level of the ecclesial communities. In addition, non-Western bishops were deeply concerned that the necessity of inculturating the message of the gospel in every cultural tradition be recognized, thus moving the Church beyond the Greco-Roman hegemony that had dominated Catholicism for centuries, even though this had produced spectacular results. This was one of the "leaps forward" that the Council was expected to make.

Another relatively important aspect was found in the office in Rome that was dedicated to missionary activity, the Congregation for the Propagation of the Faith. In this regard the discussion inexplicably focused upon a document different from the one prepared by the commission. In keeping with the will of many of the fathers, this alternative document provided for the creation of a new body for missionary activity. But "with the stroke of a pen," as one would say in a parliamentary context, the congregation was confirmed, on the contrary, as the only dicastery with competency in the area of missionary initiatives, although with a proviso for the inclusion among its leadership of some local bishops designated by the missionary episcopate. The schema was approved in a vote on October 12.

While the discussion on missionary activity was still taking place, the assembly approved *Perfectae Caritatis* (*Decree on the Appropriate Renewal of the Religious Life*), *Optatam Totius* (*Decree on Priestly Formation*) (October 11), *Gravissimum Educationis* (*Declaration on Christian Education*), and *Nostra Aetate*, which had begun as a document on relations with the Jews but had been expanded into the *Declaration on the Relationship of the Church to the Non-Christian Religions* (October 14–15). Given the fast pace of this fourth phase of activity and the approach of the next solemn session, which was scheduled for October 28, the assembly also examined the *Decree on the Ministry and Life of Priests* (*Presbyterorum Ordinis*) from October 13 to 16. So, during the next solemn session, the Council's seventh, it was possible to approve three decrees and two declarations (*declaration* being used for topics that were either too controversial or too insignificant to be the object of a formal decree).

The decree on the bishops, *Christus Dominus*, was approved, with 2,319 votes in favor, 1 opposed, and 1 abstention. Its aim was to elaborate the practical consequences of the theological principles sanctioned by *Lumen Gentium* and extensively cited in the text of the decree.[5] It acknowledged the importance, or the (relative) autonomy and self-sufficiency, of the local Church (the diocese) as an authentic realization of the universal Church.

It provided for an age limit for bishops and gave a significant boost to the episcopal conferences, to which Paul VI had referred in his institution of the synod of bishops, which was explicitly evoked in the decree:

> Bishops chosen from different parts of the world in a manner and according to a system determined or to be determined by the Roman Pontiff will render to the Supreme Pastor a more effective auxiliary service in a Council which shall be known by the special name of Synod of Bishops. This Council, as it will be representative of the whole Catholic episcopate, will bear testimony to the participation of all the bishops in hierarchical communion in the care of the universal Church. (*CD*, 5)

Christus Dominus also expressed a hope for the Roman Curia's reorganization, including representation of the bishops from the different parts of the Church. The decree recalled that

> from the earliest ages of the Church, bishops in charge of particular Churches, inspired by a spirit of fraternal charity and by zeal for the universal mission entrusted to the apostles, have pooled their resources and their aspirations in order to promote both the common good and the good of individual Churches. With this end in view, synods, provincial councils, and finally plenary councils were established in which the bishops determined on a common program to be followed in various Churches both for teaching the truths of the faith and for regulating ecclesiastical discipline.
>
> This sacred ecumenical synod expresses its earnest hope that these admirable institutions—synods and councils—may flourish with renewed vigor so that the growth of religion and the maintenance of discipline in the various Churches may increasingly be more effectively provided for in accordance with the needs of the times. (*CD*, 36)

After serious struggles and difficulties, the decree on religious life, *Perfectae Caritatis*, was approved with 2,325 votes in favor and 4 against. This decree pointed to the ideal of perfection enunciated in chapter IV of *Lumen Gentium*, making an effort to present some ways of putting this into practice. More than anything else, the orders and religious families received from this a profound impulse to reexamine their condition and proceed with concrete reforms, a process that was not without the risk of both internal tensions and tension with the Holy See.

The decree on priestly formation, *Optatam Totius*, was approved with 2,318 votes in favor and 3 against. This would turn out to be one of the documents least adequate for the real needs of the Church, not only because it was unable to explore the glaring and controversial difficulty of ecclesiastical celibacy, but especially because the Council lacked a clear understanding of the serious identity crisis that had been undermining priestly formation and the priestly state for decades, and which would manifest itself in its full gravity during the second half of the 1960s.

The declaration on Christian education, *Gravissumum Educationis* (2,290 votes in favor, 35 opposed) was the result of seven consecutive revisions, which bore witness to the difficulty of elaborating a conciliar decision on a topic characterized by wide regional variations and conditioned by an exclusive concentration on Catholic schools, while most Catholics attended or taught in secular schools. Finally, the declaration on the Church's relations with non-Christian religions, *Nostra Aetate*, was approved with 2,221 votes in favor, 88 against, and 1 abstention. In spite of the tensions that it had raised and the imperfections that remained in it, it signaled an important shift in the Catholic attitude toward other religions in general, and especially toward Judaism. The Council recognized:

> In this age of ours, when men are drawn more closely together and the bonds of friendship between different peoples are being strengthened, the Church examines with greater care the relation which she has to non-Christian religions. Ever aware of her duty to foster unity and charity among individuals, and even among nations, she reflects at the outset on what men have in common and what tends to promote fellowship among them. (*NA*, 1)

According to one particularly rich passage:

> Sounding the depths of the mystery which is the Church, this sacred Council remembers the spiritual ties which link the people of the New Covenant to the stock of Abraham.
>
> The Church of Christ acknowledges that in God's plan of salvation the beginning of her faith and election is to be found in the patriarchs, Moses and the prophets. She professes that all Christ's faithful, who as men of faith are sons of Abraham (cf. Gal. 3:7), are included in the same patriarch's call and that the salvation of the Church is mystically prefigured in the exodus of God's chosen people from land of bondage . . . The Church believes that Christ who is our peace has through his cross reconciled Jews and Gentiles and made them one in himself (cf. Eph. 2:14–16) . . .
>
> Since Christians and Jews have such a common spiritual heritage, this sacred Council wishes to encourage and further mutual understanding and appreciation. This can be obtained, especially, by way of biblical and theological enquiry and through friendly discussions.
>
> Even though the Jewish authorities and those who follow their lead pressed for the death of Christ (cf. John 19:6), neither all Jews indiscriminately at that time, nor Jews today, can be charged with the crimes committed during his passion. (*NA*, 4)

Anti-Semitism would no longer be able to claim any sort of theological legitimacy. The great wave of the Holocaust had reached all the way to St. Peter's!

The Bible and the Church

There was still an imposing quantity of work to be done during the last five weeks. The most prominent feature on the agenda was the schema of the Constitution on the Church in the Modern World. The day after the solemn session the assembly, before suspending its work for ten days in order to intensify the work of the commissions, voted on the document on revelation. The tenacious opposition to this project inspired by adherence to the Council of Trent had been overcome by a letter Paul VI had sent on October 18 to Cardinal Ottaviani, the president of the Doctrinal Commission. The infallibility of scripture had been better defined, and the assertion had been made in regard to scripture and tradition that "the Church does not derive its certainty on all revealed truth from Scripture alone." The crucial Lutheran proposition of *sola scriptura* was accepted, but not without qualification.

At the resumption of work in the hall, it was decided on November 9, 1965—partly to keep the assembly busy while the commissions were still working—that the representatives of the episcopal conferences should express their opinions on the project for reforming the discipline of indulgences, which had been prepared by the Apostolic Penitentiary. The authors of the document had not wanted to face the theological problem of indulgences, and so they had limited themselves to making a few cosmetic changes, such as the abolition of defining indulgences in concrete temporal terms (for example, 200 days, 300 days), and to the attempt to establish a greater connection between the merit acquired through the indulgence and the believer's interior disposition in performing the prayer or action in question.

The discussion immediately raised the question of the theological foundation of indulgences, which had been a source of conflict with the Protestant Reformers since the sixteenth century, and thus also a source of harm to Christian unity. It was an occasion to express the need to pass beyond the teaching and practice of indulgences as these had developed in the medieval Church. The spokesmen of the episcopal conferences, from Patriarch Maximos IV to Cardinals Alfrink, Döpfner, and König, voiced serious reservations about the project, observing that the problems related to sin and its punishment cannot be resolved with purely legal concepts, and far less with quantitative criteria. What was supposed to have been simply a meeting held to pass the time became in reality a fruitful and extremely lively dialogue. In yet another case it had become clear that there was a need for theological reformulation that could not be replaced by disciplinary adjustments. Given the way the discussion was heading, it was interrupted on November 13 with an invitation to those who had not yet been able to speak to send in their written opinions, which caused some disappointment and frustration.

Meanwhile, on November 9 there had been a vote of approval for the schema on the apostolate of the laity, and another on November 12 and 13 for the schema on the priestly ministry. Finally, on November 15, the examination of schema XIII began again. The commission had analyzed more than three thousand amendments, and so the text that was presented had been significantly modified. Not even the Council majority knew quite what to make of it. The project seemed wordy (it ran to approximately one hundred printed pages) as a result of its predominantly descriptive sociological approach. But it also seemed to have been inspired by the rather superficial optimism typical of the socioeconomic configuration of Western Europe and North America during those years. Taking a position against the schema was not an option, however, because this would mean a refusal of the spirit of concern for humanity that had inspired the creation of the document and had created great expectations in public opinion. Further, the calendar for the last weeks of the Council's work did not provide for any more pauses.

Another solemn session was held on November 18 for the approval of two other documents, the *Dogmatic Constitution on Divine Revelation, Dei Verbum* (approved with 2,344 votes in favor and 6 opposed), and the *Decree on the Apostolate of the Laity, Apostolicam Actuositatem* (2,340 votes in favor, 2 against). In his address the pope made two announcements of uncommon significance. After expressing again his highest praise for the Roman Curia, with the assurance that there was no need for structural changes but only for some improvements—which altered the Council's expectations of a profound reform—Paul VI expressed his decision to restructure the most frequently discussed congregation, the Holy Office, which would be renamed and would be governed by a new set of statutes. The Council was informed on that same occasion that causes for beatification would be opened for the two immediate predecessors of Pope Paul VI: Pius XII and John XXIII. The requests for a conciliar canonization had—significantly—been diverted into the usual bureaucratic channel. Was this the foretaste of a return to business as usual after the Council?

The constitution on revelation, *Dei Verbum*, was of exceptional theological and pastoral significance. Developed over six chapters, it focused upon the central importance of the word of God, essentially contained in the Bible, for Christian life. The sacred synod, "the living teaching office of the Church" (10), places itself beneath the word of God; above all, it listens to it itself and then proclaims it because "it wants the whole world to hear the summons to salvation, so that through hearing it may believe, through belief it may hope, through hope it may come to love" (1). The richness and complexity of *Dei Verbum* derive from its joining of the pastoral and doctrinal perspectives.

Chapter III affirms the history of biblical exegesis, which since the beginning of the modern period in the West has implied using the method of historical criticism. The singular role of the scriptures and their freedom from error are affirmed. Nonetheless, understanding the Bible as a historical book requires the participation of the community of believers in addition to the collaboration of the bishops and theologians.

One of the key concepts of the document is the "economy" of revelation (chapters IV and V): the preparation for the coming of Christ, the fullness of revelation, has its roots in the account of salvation told in the Hebrew scriptures:

> God, the inspirer and author of the books of both Testaments, in his wisdom has so brought it about that the New should be hidden in the Old and that the Old should be made manifest in the New . . . The Word of God, which is the power of God for salvation to everyone who has faith (cf. Rom. 1:16), is set forth and displays its power in a most wonderful way in the writings of the New Testament. (16–17)

Dei Verbum, finally, situates the scriptures within the life of the Church (14–15). All Christians are urgently invited to read the scriptures—citing St. Jerome's aphorism, "ignorance of the scriptures is ignorance of Christ." The work of the exegetes and theologians is at the service of the word. Central importance is given to the parallel between the table of the word and that of the body of Christ, a comparison that John XXIII loved to make and that was solemnly affirmed in the *Constitution on the Sacred Liturgy*. *Dei Verbum* stated: "The Church has always venerated the divine Scriptures as she venerated the Body of the Lord, in so far as she never ceases, particularly in the sacred liturgy, to partake of the bread of life and to offer it to the faithful from the one table of the Word of God and the Body of Christ" (21).

Finally, after the cautions and limitations imposed by the Council of Trent and after the marginalization of scripture in the Catholic community resulting from the Counter-Reformation, the Roman Church was rediscovering a proper awareness of its submission to the word of God. The delicate relationship between the Bible and tradition, which the Council declined to specify in a formula, was brought back into a perspective of a dynamic interaction, summoning Christian reflection and ecclesial experience to further exploration.[6]

The decree on the laity, *Apostolicam Actuositatem*, heralded the arrival of the important movement for the promotion of the laity that had permeated contemporary Catholicism and enlivened it on many fronts.

Nevertheless, the document was still a prisoner of the distinction between the laity and the clergy and seemed to be filled with attempts to justify the laity against the clergy. The decree is articulated in six chapters and begins by evoking the theological foundations of the participation of lay people in the mission of the Church. It then indicates the aims of the lay apostolate, emphasizing the "renewal of the temporal order," and describes the different areas of this apostolic endeavor and the forms that it can assume. Here the document demonstrates a completely "Roman" perspective in giving pride of place to the group Catholic Action. Finally, it restates the subordination of lay people to the hierarchy and the necessity of their being formed for the apostolate. In the end, the decree was unable to penetrate the vision of the Church formulated in *Lumen Gentium*, which focused upon the people of God rather than the laity and failed to take into account the spheres of action that a rediscovered understanding of the universal priesthood would open up to all the members of the Church within ecclesial life itself, and not only in regard to the temporal order.

Christians Live within History

After the November 19 vote on the Declaration on Religious Freedom, the work of the assembly was again interrupted until November 30 in order to permit the commissions to move forward in their examination and integration of the amendments to be made to the remaining schemata (one declaration, two decrees, and one constitution). This interruption was necessary to permit a vote on December 2 on the schema concerning the ministry and life of priests, which was still the object of great dissatisfaction. It gave the impression of having been created to satisfy complaints from the clergy that they were being overlooked rather than as a mature and deliberate act. On December 6 the 168th and final working session, it was also possible to take a vote on the document on the Church in the modern world, *Gaudium et Spes*. On this occasion the greatest number of opposing votes were cast on the sections relating to marriage (140) and peace (144), which were evidently still unsatisfactory.

With its ninth solemn session on December 7, 1965, Vatican II concluded its work by approving the *Declaration on Religious Freedom, Dignitatis Humanae* (2,308 votes in favor, 70 against, 6 abstentions); the *Decree on the Missionary Activity of the Church, Ad Gentes* (2,394 votes in favor, 5 against); the *Decree on the Ministry and Life of Priests, Presbyterorum Ordinis* (2,390 votes in favor, 4 against); and finally, the *Pastoral Constitution on the Church in the Modern World, Gaudium et Spes* (2,309 votes in favor, 75 against, 7 abstentions).

On that same occasion there was a simultaneous proclamation at St. Peter's and in Istanbul of the mutual lifting of the excommunications that had been exchanged almost a thousand years earlier (in 1054) between the

Churches of Constantinople and Rome. The act signified the willingness on the part of Christians and their Churches to overcome their ancient dissensions, free themselves from the restrictions and misfortunes of the past, and take up a constructive fraternal dialogue for the sake of unity.

The *Declaration on Religious Freedom (Dignitatis Humanae)* had survived great tension and uncertainty and was still characterized by a rhetorical approach that wavered between theological and purely rational expression, but it was a profound innovation for the modern Catholic attitude, recognizing the validity of complete freedom of conscience on both the individual and collective level. In *Dignitatis Humanae* Vatican Council II began by acknowledging that

> contemporary man is becoming increasingly conscious of the dignity of the human person; more and more people are demanding that men should exercise fully their own judgment and a responsible freedom in their actions and should not be subject to the pressure of coercion but be inspired by a sense of duty. At the same time they are demanding constitutional limitation of the powers of government to prevent excessive restriction of the rightful freedom of individuals and associations. This demand for freedom in human society is concerned chiefly with man's spiritual values, and especially with what concerns the free practice of religion in society.
>
> This sacred Council begins by professing that God himself has made known to the human race how men by serving him can be saved and reach happiness in Christ. We believe that this one true religion continues to exist in the Catholic and Apostolic Church, to which the Lord Jesus entrusted the task of spreading it among all men . . . All men are bound to seek the truth, especially in what concerns God and his Church, and to embrace it and hold on to it as they come to know it.
>
> The sacred Council likewise proclaims that these obligations bind man's conscience. Truth can impose itself on the mind of man only in virtue of its own truth, which wins over the mind with both gentleness and power. (*DH*, 1)

With this act, the Council overcame the habitual exclusive defense of the *libertas ecclesiae* and the accompanying distinction between *hypothesis* (freedom for Catholics when they are in the minority) and *thesis* (the intransigence of Catholics when they are in the majority), not to mention the presumption of defending truth from error by punishing the errant.[7]

Dignitatis Humanae developed in its essence the teaching formulated by John XXIII in 1963 in the final section of *Pacem in Terris*. By developing the teaching on religious liberty the Council gave theological depth to the proclamation of human rights. *Dignitatis Humanae* undoubtedly represents an important moment in the process of evangelizing modern culture when it asserts that

> one of the key truths in Catholic teaching, a truth that is contained in the word of God and constantly preached by the Fathers, is that man's response to God by faith ought to be free, and that therefore nobody is to be forced to embrace the faith against his will. The act of faith is of its very nature a free act. Man, redeemed by Christ the Savior and called through Jesus Christ to be an adopted son of God, cannot give his adherence to God when he reveals himself unless, drawn by the Father, he submits to God with a faith that is reasonable and free. It is therefore fully in accordance with the nature of faith that in religious matters every form of coercion by men should be excluded. Consequently the principle of religious liberty contributes in no small way to the development of the situation in which men can without hindrance be invited to the Christian faith, embrace it of their own free will and give it practical expression in every sphere of their lives. (*DH*, 10)

At the same time, the Council clarified the public conditions that must be in place for the urgent dialogue between religion and modernity. In order to develop this, dialogue needs public religious freedom and support from law. By demonstrating the religious foundation of liberty, the Council fathers also showed other religions one possible model for approaching the idea of religious freedom, each religion beginning from its own roots and preserving its specific identity and mission.

Nevertheless, the clear distinction between the sphere of law, with its sense of obligation, and the religious sphere, with the freedom of faith, held consequences—some of them troubling—for relations *within* the Church (the acknowledgment of a relationship of communion or of excommunication) and for questions of faith and the obligations deriving from the faith (the personal condition of "orthodoxy" or "heterodoxy").

The *Decree on the Missionary Activity of the Church (Ad Gentes)* laid out in six chapters the criteria for a radical renewal of missionary spirit and activity. Its goal was replacing the delegation of responsibility for mission to a small professional minority, typical of the colonial period in the West, by an affirmation of the missionary nature of the entire Church. Transformations had been taking place in missionary experience in Latin America, Africa, and Asia, where a rapid abandonment of the colonial period was under way. The countries of the earliest period of evangelization were reeling from the effects of dechristianization. Both found in this document a significant echo and affirmation, made possible by the ecclesiological premises established in the *Constitution on the Sacred Liturgy* and the *Dogmatic Constitution on the Church*.

One of the crucial assertions in *Ad Gentes* (19) stated:

This work of implanting the Church in a particular human community reaches a definite point when the assembly of the faithful, already rooted in the social life of the people and to some extent con-
formed to its culture, enjoys a certain stability and performance; when
it has its own priests, although insufficient, its own religious and laity, and possesses those ministries and institutions which are required
for leading and spreading the life the people of God under the leadership of their own bishop.

In *Ad Gentes* (22) the Council showed great trust in its conviction that

the seed which is the word of God grows out of good soil watered
by the divine dew, it absorbs moisture, transforms it, and makes it
part of itself, so that eventually it bears much fruit. So too indeed,
just as happened in the economy of the incarnation, the young
Churches, which are rooted in Christ and built on the foundations
of the apostles, take over all the riches of the nations which have
been given to Christ as an inheritance. They borrow from the cus-
toms, traditions, wisdom, teaching, arts and sciences of their people
everything which could be used to praise the glory of the Creator,
manifest the grace of the savior, or contribute to the right ordering
of Christian life.

In these young Churches the Christian life of the people of God must be
renewed according to the norms of the Council and reach maturity in every area. The faithful, with growing self-awareness, must become a living
community of faith, liturgy, and charity. The laity, through civic and apostolic activity, should strive to create an order of justice and charity in their
cities. The communications media should be used in an appropriate and
prudent manner, and families, practicing a truly Christian form of life,
should become places of formation for the lay apostolate and for priestly
and religious vocations. The bishops of the Third World had made a decisive, if inconspicuous, contribution to the success of this emphasis on spiritual renewal, opening up perspectives that just a few years earlier had been
thought to belong to a few groups of the avant garde.

Like the *Decree on Priestly Formation (Apostolicam Actuositatem)*, the *Decree on the Ministry and Life of Priests (Presbyterorum Ordinis)* suffered from
the lack of adequate reflection on the state of the priesthood. There was
also no concrete model to follow, especially after the controversial experience of the worker-priests in France. The Council was unaware of how
quickly the incipient crisis would be triggered by social changes and by the
transition from a "cleric-dominated" Church to a community of the people
of God. From the very moment of their approval, the three chapters of the

decree already seemed dated and devoid of any impulse capable of guiding future developments.

The Council had concluded its work with the approval of the *Pastoral Constitution on the Church in the Modern World (Gaudium et Spes)*, the only document composed entirely during the Council itself. The constitution was composed of nine chapters, two prefaces, an introduction, and a conclusion. An explanatory note clarified the meaning of the description "pastoral" as applied to the document, asserting that "on the basis of doctrinal principles, the constitution intends to present the Church's relationship with the world and the people of today." The first four chapters were dedicated to "the teaching on the human person, on the world in which the human person lives, and on the Church's relationship to these realities." The remaining five chapters made "a closer examination of the various aspects of modern life and human society, especially the questions and problems that seem to be most urgent." The constitution opened with a sweeping preface declaring that

> the joy and hope, the grief and anguish of the men of our time, especially of those who are poor or afflicted in any way, are the joy and hope, the grief and anguish of the followers of Christ as well. Nothing that is genuinely human fails to find an echo in their hearts. For theirs is a community composed of men, of men who, united in Christ and guided by the holy Spirit, press onwards towards the kingdom of the Father and are bearers of a message of salvation intended for all men. That is why Christians cherish a feeling of deep solidarity with the human race and its history. (*GS*, 1).

It acknowledged:

> At all times the Church carries the responsibility of reading the signs of the time and of interpreting them in the light of the Gospel, if it is to carry out its task. In language intelligible to every generation, she should be able to answer the ever recurring questions which men ask about the meaning of this present life and of the life to come, and how one is related to the other. We must be aware of and understand the aspirations, the yearnings, and the often dramatic features of the world in which we live. (*GS*, 4)

> The people of God believes that it is led by the Spirit of the Lord who fills the whole world. Moved by that faith it tries to discern in the events, the needs, and the longings which it shares with other men of our time, what may be genuine signs of the presence or of the purpose of God. For faith throws a new light on all things and makes known the full ideal which God has set for man, thus guiding the mind towards solutions that are fully human. (*GS*, 11)

In addition to this recognition of the value of human history, the constitution also admits that the Church

> is not unaware how much it has profited from the history and development of mankind. It profits from the experience of past ages, from the progress of the sciences, and from the riches hidden in various cultures, through which greater light is thrown on the nature of man and new avenues to truth are opened up ... The Church itself also recognizes that it has benefited and is still benefiting from the opposition of its enemies and persecutors. (*GS*, 44)

Returning to the guidelines set forth in Pope John XXIII's encyclical *Pacem in Terris*, the Council recalls that

> it is of supreme importance, especially in a pluralistic society, to work out a proper vision of the relationship between the political community and the Church, and to distinguish clearly between the activities of Christians, acting individually or collectively in their own name as citizens guided by the dictates of a Christian conscience, and their activity acting along with their pastors in the name of the Church.
>
> The Church, by reason of her role and competence, is not identified with any political community nor bound by ties to any political system. It is at once the sign and the safeguard of the transcendental dimension of the human person.
>
> The political community and the Church are autonomous and independent of each other in their own fields. Nevertheless, both are devoted to the personal vocation of man, though under different titles. (*GS*, 76)

The final topic, which was the most heated, given the bloody conflict taking place in Southeast Asia, was that of the legitimacy or illegitimacy of war. The constitution acknowledges that the Council is obliged to make

> a completely fresh reappraisal of war. Men of this generation should realize that they will have to render an account of their warlike behavior; the destiny of generations to come depends largely on the decisions they make today.
>
> With these considerations in mind the Council, endorsing the condemnations of total warfare issued by recent popes, declares: Every act of war directed to the indiscriminate destruction of whole cities or vast areas with their inhabitants is a crime against God and man, which merits firm and unequivocal condemnation. (*GS*, 80)

It was the most that the Council majority was able to say.

The interweaving between theological considerations and sociological arguments, between evangelical optimism and naive faith in progress was not totally overcome insofar as it was an expression of the different mind-sets present not only in the Council but also within the majority itself. The clear and farsighted identification of the crucial issues for contemporary society and for Christian witness within society (human dignity, the family, culture, economic life, poverty, and peace) might have been more penetrating if it had been accompanied by brief citations from the gospel. Instead, it was watered down with long and context-dependent considerations of social philosophy, constituting a sort of revenge of "social doctrine," which *Gaudium et Spes* had passed beyond in so many ways.

And yet much credit is due to the bishops and theologians who made such great efforts on this project, with the support of Paul VI. It must also be emphasized that in the period after the Council every significant controversy that took place in the Church was closely connected with the assertions found in *Gaudium et Spes*—from the discussions begun by the encyclical *Humane Vitae* (on birth control) to the controversies over liberation theology, and many others. All of them have their roots in the *Pastoral Constitution on the Church in the Modern World*. This is an indication of how frequently the document touched a nerve in Christian experience and witness.

Among several of the Council's other achievements worth mentioning are its refusal to reiterate the condemnation of Marxism and communism—which would have seemed "prehistoric" after just a few years—and its effort to pass beyond those lists of norms relating to social conduct that, beginning with *Rerum Novarum* (Pope Leo XIII's 1891 encyclical letter on the problems of the working class), had always been derived from abstract general principles through deductive reasoning. A renewed appreciation of human history permitted the Council to propose an inductive method using the major events taking place ("the signs of the times") to formulate criteria of behavior, as seen also in the encyclicals of Pope John.

There is a striking disparity among the various acts approved in this fourth period of work. The level and impact of the topics considered vary greatly, and the extent of their elaboration and their consistency with the basic approach of Vatican II is conspicuously uneven. The decision of Paul VI to create a synod of bishops[8]—a body that would meet periodically but would not be permanent, and would be a consultative assembly without power of decision—took the form of a pontifical act, but it must be recognized as a result of the last phase of the Council. The request for a central collegial body that would regularly help the Bishop of Rome in the exercise of responsibilities for guiding the universal Church seemed to have been accepted. Only subsequent experience would tell how many would or would not complain that what the pope had created had fallen short of what the Council had asked. But this was, in any case, an absolute novelty, which found only a remote comparison in the Consistory of Cardinals, which from the eleventh to the fourteenth century had met frequently with the pope to examine and decide upon major problems. It would not be rash to assert that the decision of Paul VI would have been unthinkable without the atmosphere and context of the Council.

The Closing of the Council

On December 8 a formal, solemn, and festive celebration of the Council's closing was held in St. Peter's Square. The ceremony included the publication of a series of messages to humanity: to politicians, thinkers, scientists, artists, workers, the poor, the sick, the suffering, and young people. The messages, which purported to speak in the name of the Council, were introduced by Paul VI himself, who said in his preface, "Before it is dissolved, the Council wishes to fulfill its prophetic role by translating the 'good news' that it has for the world into brief messages composed in language understandable to all." But the messages had not been either composed or approved by the Council. They were the work of the pope and his collaborators.

The apostolic letter of Paul VI *In Spiritu Sancto* arranged for the closing of the Council and expressed again his full approval of what the assembly had decided, with the request that all of the faithful show reverent obedience for these decisions. In comparison with both the Council of Trent and Vatican Council I, at the conclusion of this Council's work there was a much more peaceful atmosphere among the bishops, who had reached almost complete unanimity. There was also greater tranquility among the faithful, who had been called to emerge from their state of passivity in order to play an active and creative role in the implementation of the Council's decisions. But in some circles—including the Bologna workshop—there was a sense of foreboding that the momentum for renewal generated by the Council and by the pontificate of John XXIII would dissipate too quickly, permitting the return of a Counter-Reformation if not an outright rebirth of the Constantinian form of Catholicism.

In fidelity to the pastoral approach outlined by John XXIII, Vatican II did not impose rigid norms or uniform standards of behavior on the Church, nor did it provide for disciplinary sanctions. Instead, it encouraged Catholicism to renew itself through a sincere evaluation of its faithfulness to the gospel, conducted in the light of faith and in response to the signs of the times. After the Council there began the long period of assimilation by the Churches and believers. Less than a month after the conclusion of Vatican II, on January 3, 1966, the Motu Proprio *Finis Concilio* created a postconciliar structure parallel to that of the Council's commissions, with the members of these same commissions forming agencies for bishops, religious, missions, education, the laity, and so on. The members of the

Board of Presidents and the Coordinating Commission were also appointed to a commission responsible for overseeing postconciliar activity and the interpretation of the Council's decisions. But no postconciliar body was created to correspond with the Doctrinal Commission of Vatican II. Doctrinal questions would return immediately to the jealous supervision of the Holy Office (now called the Sacred Congregation for the Doctrine of the Faith). This was inspired by the concern to make provisions for institutions and criteria to guide the interpretation and implementation of the Council's decisions. It indicated that both the assembly and the Apostolic See wanted the Council's work to be continued. But at the same time, it showed that there was a certain preference in Rome for a centrally controlled implementation. The motivation for this seemed clear: the Council was nothing more and nothing less than the sum total of its decisions, and the effect of these decisions would depend upon their being situated within the existing framework of Catholicism, and especially of its center in Rome.

During the decade after the end of Vatican II the commissions mentioned above disappeared into oblivion without ever having functioned; instead, a mechanical vision of implementing the Council based upon understanding of and commentary upon the official documents dominated. The books dedicated to these commentaries make up a substantial library. In most cases the commentaries were written by the same theologians who had directly collaborated in the creation of the Council documents, so the point of view is the same.

When the Council fathers left Rome at the end of 1965, was the world any different than in October 1962? Had the context of Christian life and the Church's activities changed? Not much time had gone by, not even forty months, and most of those present for the opening of Vatican II were still active. Even so, quite a bit had happened. Humanity's mastery of space had increased exponentially: probes had been sent to the moon, others had gone out toward Mars, and astronauts had entered outer space. The Cold War seemed to be intensifying and expanding. In the Far East, in what appeared to be the ultimate subversion of power, China had begun its Cultural Revolution, while Southeast Asia saw an intensification of the conflict in Vietnam with increasing U.S. military involvement. This involvement had unleashed a growing reaction from young people; demonstrations in the major universities of North America would soon pass beyond simple protests against the military intervention of their country to radical protest that would flood all of the West.

It is difficult to know how much those emerging from the atmosphere of the Council knew about these deep changes. The world that they had left behind in 1962 to set out on the adventure of the Council had changed considerably. This created unexpected problems and challenges and, above all, threatened to make the decisions of the Council outdated, the outcome of a cultural and social context undergoing rapid transformation.

The bishops themselves had also changed. Participating in the Council had made an authentic spiritual impact on many of them. It had influenced their personalities and even brought about a few fairly surprising "conversions." Pietro Parente's change of heart on the issue of episcopal collegiality had made a huge impression, as he had been one of the main exponents of the Holy Office view. One could also consider the cases of Canada's Cardinal Léger and Cardinals Lercaro and Motolese of Italy. Each of them, in his own way, experienced the Council as a spiritual event that demanded a radical modification of how he fulfilled his ministry as a bishop.

In April 1966 Léger wrote, "One can say that the Council meant nothing to him if it did not convert him, if it did not change his life, if it did not bring to life unknown or neglected responsibilities." The following year he went to Africa to share the suffering of the lepers. Lercaro dedicated himself to a profound reform of the Diocese of Bologna and to a radical testimony on behalf of peace. Motolese experienced a doctrinal "conversion," forsaking the conservative attitude that he had maintained during the Council. There was even talk of a conversion of Hélder Câmara.

The experience of liturgical reform brought to light how the reception of Vatican II would differ according to the conditions prevailing before the Council and how these had changed by the time it ended. Just as Vatican II had been the synthesis of a great variety of contributions, so now it would take on a variety of accents in the Churches that were called to assimilate it. The idea of an ordered, uniform implementation directed by Rome was not realistic, although the bureaucracy continued to favor it. To imagine that central postconciliar structures could guide the implementation was not only self-deluding, but it demonstrated a new perspective of Church centralization that was inconsistent with Vatican II itself.

The Church would also need to face the topics that the Council had remained silent on, from the ends of marriage and procreation to priestly celibacy and the poverty of the Church. The satisfaction and enthusiasm of the final days had perhaps hidden from most of the participants the difficulties that would soon surface in translating the Council's impulses into the concrete life of the Church. But, as with every significant step in life, maybe it was necessary to underestimate the problems that would follow in order to avoid the risk of paralysis. As before the Council, and even more so now, the Church of Vatican II, faithful to the impulse from which it drew its very existence, looked forward with courage and optimism, without letting itself be limited even by the understandable and perhaps inevitable risks.

6

For the Renewal of Christianity

To what sort of Council did Pope John want to give birth? He had not hesitated at all to characterize the Council in an absolutely traditional manner, that is, as an assembly composed solely of the bishops. But this does not contradict the fact that he wanted the Council to inaugurate a new era, to introduce the perennial Church to a new phase of its journey. From this perspective the Council assumed a unique importance, and much more so as an event than as a means for the elaboration and production of norms, as had been the case for the assemblies of past centuries.

The Council was intended to be a "flash of sublime illumination," as Pope John had said on a number of occasions. He had also referred to it as a new Pentecost. It was an exalted way of emphasizing, in characteristically Christian terms, the exceptional nature of that historical juncture and the extraordinary perspectives that it opened up. So the Church needed to face the necessity of a profound renewal, so that it could present itself to the world and communicate the message of the gospel to humanity with the same power and immediacy as at the first Pentecost. The reference to Pentecost, moreover, brought to the forefront the action of the Holy Spirit rather than that of the pope, the Church, or even the Council assembly itself.

A thorough evaluation of the Council's results requires complex analysis on many levels. One reasonable approach might be to compare the atmosphere during the preparation for the Council (January 1959 to October 1962) with the atmosphere at its conclusion in December 1965. In spite of the flood of secularization that had taken place, at least in the West, John XXIII's announcement had unleashed a great outpouring of attention and interest on the part of the public. But the announcement had been as vague as it was exciting, and so it had raised a number of questions about the future Council.

In 1959 at least two authoritative personalities and one influential group already had composed and circulated some notes about the upcoming Council. These were Swiss theologian Otto Karrer, Jesuit Cardinal Augustin Bea, and the directive committee of the Catholic Conference for Ecumenical

119

Questions. The three documents expressed a modest ecumenical optimism while warning against actions of the Council, such as doctrinal definitions or condemnations, that might disappoint their hopes. What they wished for instead were actions that would smooth the way toward reconciliation, and union, such as an emphasis on communion over legalism, a reduction of centralization, and the recognition of the centrality of the Bible.

A Retrospective Preparation?

What followed was the long period of preparation, which was dominated by the gathering of opinions from the bishops and the creation of the complex machine of preparatory commissions that would produce more than seventy project outlines that would be submitted to the Council. But neither the world's bishops nor the central preparatory bodies had the will or the energy to formulate a comprehensive plan for the future assembly as a whole. Almost all of the schemata submitted to the Council were summaries of the most recent papal teaching. They were more a compendium of the past than a response to current problems.

For his part, John XXIII's charismatic approach was almost a technique of education by stages. His sole concern was to propose to all—bishops, members of the Curia, and ordinary Christians—powerful guidelines ("renewal," "the pastoral approach," "signs of the times," "peace") inspired both by the faith and by history's critical juncture, with a profound trust in the Holy Spirit, in the Church's inherent sense of faith, and in the creative capacity of the assembly of bishops. The long span of time between the announcement in 1959 and the beginning of work in the fall of 1962 undeniably had a positive effect. It prompted and sharpened the expectations that made Vatican II an event that involved countless people, who perceived it as something belonging to them.

The Church was invited to recognize that it was facing a new world before which it must represent the values of universal equality, poverty, justice, peace, and Christian unity. The Council, then, was called to be a "face to face encounter with the risen Christ." But even on the occasion of this message (September 11, 1962), the pope did not dictate the order of the day for the Council's work but instead forcefully outlined an extraordinarily sweeping perspective. Thirty days later the opening speech, Gaudet Mater Ecclesia, far from being an incidental message, gave him the opportunity to indicate the spirit, aims, and limits of the Council. Vatican II's duty would not be "solely that of preserving this valuable treasure [of tradition], as if we were only concerned about times long past, but that of dedicating ourselves with ready willingness and without fear to the work required by our age."

In the light of the historical context, the pope stated that the Council was essentially "a leap forward toward an assimilation of doctrine and a formation of consciences." He even indicated a methodology, according to which it would be necessary to distinguish between "the substance of ancient doctrine . . . and the manner of presenting it." This is how the pope emphasized the profound difference between the central contents of Christian revelation (the incarnation, the cross, the resurrection, the Trinity, and so on) and the ways in which people throughout the ages have expressed these in the words and concepts of their time. The contents were unchangeable, but the presentation had to be updated. This was, at the same time, both less and more than a plan of action. It was the attitude that the pope proposed for the Council fathers, while leaving them full freedom and complete responsibility in their role as protagonists of the Council. Just a few days after the beginning of the Council, Cardinal Bea, who had understood sooner and better than anyone else the full significance of the pope's speech, presented a true plan for the Council. It summarized the speech point by point and came to the conclusion that the number of doctrinal schemata should be reduced and that they should be reformulated in a way consistent with the pope's proposals. A couple of days later Cardinal Montini went to Cardinal Cicognani, the Secretary of

Photograph reproduced by courtesy of Giuseppe Alberigo

Giuseppe Alberigo, speaking on December 12, 1985, on the occasion of a colloquium held at Assisi on the topic "Twenty Years since Vatican II," during the preparation of the five-volume project that he headed which produced *History of Vatican II* (Orbis Books, 1995–2006).

State, with a long and substantial letter on the "lack of an overall plan for the Council." The Archbishop of Milan, Montini, echoed the plan that Cardinal Suenens of Belgium had submitted to the pope, according to which the Council should work along two main lines: the Church within itself and in its relations with society. Montini's letter went on to recommend mediation to save some of the preparatory schemata from being thrown away.

While these proposals were still unknown to most, the Council assembly approved a message to humanity expressing the bishops' commitment to become ever more faithful witnesses to the gospel of Christ through a renewal of both themselves and the Church, in order that "the light of the faith may shine forth more clearly and brightly," bringing "into our hearts the anxieties of all peoples, their anguish of body and soul, their suffering, desires, and hopes." The message was intended to express the Church's affinity for all of humanity and also to contest the lack of concern for the world shown in the preparatory schemata.

Initial Bearings

Although a true plan for Vatican II had not been formulated, important indications had emerged, in the first place, for the practical possibility of an ecumenical perspective, with the corollary of a refusal to issue condemnations. It would also be necessary to reconsider the theology on the Church, moving beyond the "fulfillment" that Vatican Council I had been portrayed as being. In addition, the question of the relationship between the bishops and the Roman Curia had been raised, as had the more controversial problem of reforming the Curia. On another front, progress was made toward recognizing the necessity for the Council to face the Church's relationship with the modern world in a perspective less narrow than that of official agreements with governments, or even that of social doctrine, precisely as the bishops had resolved to do in the message they released at the beginning of the Council. Vatican II would move forward in realizing a compromise between the vast horizons opened within the bishops' minds by John XXIII's opening speech and the series of "minor" problems that the bishops themselves had expressed in the survey taken of them, and which had generated projects by the dozen.

John XXIII's wager on an independent Council that would not be directed from above by the Curia produced great results, although these came at a price. In reviewing the work of the Council and rereading the documents that the assembly produced, one comes across a few major steps forward—which were as unpredictable as they were decisive—toward a greater assimilation of essential Christian teaching and a formulation of this teaching more in keeping with pastoral needs. But there are also some glaring gaps and omissions. The most notable of these concerns responsibility toward poor peoples and the poverty of the Church. This theme, already contained in Suenens's plan, had been repeated by the pope during two addresses, in September and October of 1962, and also by the Council fathers in their opening message. After Paul VI retired the use of the tiara in November 1964, with the Council's work about to close, a few hundred of the bishops—moved both by the importance of the subject and by the meager acceptance it had found—signed a series of thirteen propositions embodying their commitment to overcome personally a lack of "poverty of life according to the gospel."[1]

The repeated expressions of hope for a reform of the Curia also produced only modest results. Other problems that did not find a place on Vatican II's agenda included racism, which was still inspiring seriously discriminatory behavior, and the question of the animist religions popular in Africa. The entire array of questions related to the place of women in the Christian community was "absorbed" within statements about the Virgin Mary.

But an overall consideration of the results of Vatican II cannot ignore certain methodological advancements that may not have been expressed in precise formulas but nevertheless had a significant impact on the discussions within the Council and underlie many of its main conclusions. It is impossible to deny that the traditional deductive method had been eclipsed, however incompletely. The progress already made in theological studies before the Council had an influence on this process, overcoming the suspicion of heterodoxy that had followed it. The Council's repeated use of an inductive approach amounted to a sea change that was sometimes opposed but was irreversible nonetheless.

Useless disputes with "profane" studies and Protestant theological reflection had long occupied Catholic theology, and papal teaching had maintained this stance, which had now been surpassed. For a number of centuries the courageous and farsighted innovation that Thomas Aquinas had introduced in the Middle Ages with the acceptance of "pagan" Aristotelianism as a basis for Christian reflection had paradoxically been seen as definitive and valid for all time. The risk of a continual reduction of doctrinal propositions to abstract formulas, with the dramatic impoverishment of the Christian message that it brought, was ignored in the name of Neo-Scholasticism. In this regard as well, the atmosphere that the Council created permitted the beginning of a renewal capable of giving breathing room to Catholic reflection and of reestablishing contact with contemporary thought.

History as Friend

Connected with the use of the inductive method was the acceptance of history, the recognition that Christianity lives and breathes within (and not outside of, or despite) the chronicle of human events. The urgency of a profound critical revision of Catholicism's attitude had already found a timid sort of expression in Pius XII's teaching that the Church should look to history. With his successor, this effort of readjustment took on unexpected momentum and immediacy. The papal declaration opening the Council emphasized the permanent relationship Christ has with human history, a relationship that is intensified in history's critical moments. The declaration went on to maintain that it is precisely in such moments that the Church must intensify its own efforts. In recalling this fundamental criterion, John XXIII applied it to his own day. He asserted that "a crisis is taking place in society," that "humanity is on the brink of a new era," and that it was passing through a particularly dense and significant phase. In these clear assessments the pope was striving to produce a comprehensive evaluation of his time rather than a sociopolitical appraisal.

Pope John concentrated upon the profound, long-term factors important for the destiny of humanity as a whole. History, as both the past and the present life of humanity, is the context for the divine plan of salvation, in which—and not in spite of which—the Christian religion unfolds. It is here that the pilgrimage of the Christian people takes place, as the *Decree on the Missionary Activity of the Church* recalls: "God decided to enter into the history of mankind in a new and definitive manner, by sending his own Son" (no. 3). In terms of the relationship between the Church and history, Vatican II on the whole radically reversed the tendency that had prevailed within Catholicism for least four centuries.

The most decisive indications of this are found in the constitutions on the liturgy, on the Church, and on the word of God. These actively demonstrate the relevance of the historical condition of Christianity. In this context a critical role was played by the insufficient and marginal place assigned to the Holy Spirit in the overall scheme of the Council. With the lack of an adequate development of this dimension, the Council's pronouncements lent themselves to simplistic interpretations that failed to grasp the real historical significance of these events and the profound, intricate meaning that they contained, which can be perceived only by moving to a different level of comprehension.

In more than one case the Council demonstrated an unimaginative application of its own criteria. This happened with its declarations on the influence of the media in modern society. It is also shown in the Council's facile acceptance of Western historical optimism throughout much of the constitution *Gaudium et Spes*, and in that same document's superficial interpretation of the rich tapestry found in the gospel that illustrates humanity's yearning for peace. It is no accident that Christian history is full of misunderstandings, in the sense both of blindness before great historical novelties and of failure to recognize the messianic significance of history itself.

Despite these shortcomings, Vatican II made it legitimate to go beyond interpreting Christianity solely within the perspective of salvation and providence and to make instead an active and positive assessment through the rigorous use of the historical-critical method.

Expectations and Results

It is interesting to emphasize the points of continuity between the expectations expressed before the Council and the results of this event. In spite of considerable correspondence between these expectations and the outcomes, it seems that Vatican II—although it was weighed down by a certain number of decrees inspired by preconciliar attitudes—mainly exceeded the expectations, accomplishing a more profound and organic transformation than observers had had the foresight and courage to hope for beforehand. This observation is not meant to deny the contribution made by the renewal movements of the first half of the twentieth century. Indeed, every time Vatican II was able to provide incisive responses to the problems that it faced, the clarity was derived from the work and experience of these movements.

The great majority of the fathers agreed with the new perspectives John XXIII had outlined on October 11, 1962. His wager on the creative possibilities of a Council placed within the hands of the bishops—amid uncertainties and inconsistencies—had paid off. A new Council had been born, one different from its historical predecessors in that it had not been determined by responses to heresies—like the ancient councils—or by the organizational needs of Christianity—like the Lateran councils of the Middle Ages—or by dramatic emergencies—like the councils of Constance, Basel, and Trent. Neither did it follow a precisely determined plan—like Vatican Council I in 1870.

The Council carried out its work during two different pontificates. John XXIII had decided upon and inaugurated it, and Paul VI had accepted, continued, and concluded it. The impulses that each of these had given to the assembly of bishops and the contributions that each had made had been noticeably different. From Pope John had come the very idea of a council characterized by "thinking big," by the conviction that the faith could generate a historical event capable of satisfying the new needs of humanity. When he decided to intervene in the work of the assembly, he did so with the desire to facilitate the manifestation of the deepest convictions of the Council fathers. Pope Paul loyally accepted the Council, made an effort to guarantee its unanimity, frequently intervened in order to moderate and restrain the convictions of most of his brother bishops, and found the tenacity to bring the Council to a conclusion.

A New Council

Vatican II presents itself as a council committed to bringing the Church to respond in a united and positive manner to the people of today, reproposing the essential contents of the gospel with pastoral sensitivity and in a modern voice. These criteria were not always consistently applied in the work and decisions of the assembly; the restricted time available made such a task very difficult, and all the more so given that these criteria had long been unfamiliar—even foreign—to Catholicism. There was a lack both of recent practice and of a thorough understanding of these principles.

The Council assembly also found sufficient courage and conviction to abandon the Eurocentrism that had characterized it at the beginning. The bishops of the Third World had gradually gained greater importance, exercising a growing influence on the work and its outcomes. This de-Europeanization found its confirmation above all in the impact that the Council had on the "periphery" of the world. The cultural and Christian experience of these bishops was decisive in reinforcing the trend toward leaving behind the legalistic approach that had characterized the Church in the West. This gave rise to Vatican II's drive to place the legal and institutional aspects of the Church beneath its sacramental dimension.

The renunciation of the image of the Church as a "perfect society" analogous to a modern state permitted the recovery of the Church's communitarian nature on all levels. It is significant that one decisive initiative in this regard came from the group of bishops from Chile, who were determined to insert within the constitution *Lumen Gentium* the crucial assertion that God has "willed to make men holy and save them, not as individuals without any bond or link between them, but rather to make them into a people who might acknowledge him and serve him in holiness" (9).

The unprecedented composition of the assembly—so numerous and highly varied—helps to explain the difficulty of creating a plan in advance for Vatican II and also explains the great improvement in quality between the preparatory formulations and the final documents, and much more so between the atmosphere of Catholicism in the 1950s and that found at the conclusion of the Council. Almost no one who heard the announcement of the new Council had been able to imagine that, instead of merely setting rules, the documents of Vatican II would point the Church in a new direction. The most that one dared hope for was that the Council would forego condemnation.

Moving beyond the period of ecclesiocentrism implied not only the decline of the Church's dominant position over the faith, but above all the rediscovery of the other dimensions of Christian life. So priorities began to be reversed, with the abandonment of references to ecclesiastical institutions and their authority and efficiency as the center and measure of the faith and the Church. What makes up the Church is, instead, faith, communion, and the willingness to serve. These are the normative values for measuring the extent to which ecclesiastical practices and institutions conform to the gospel. Rethinking and overturning priorities imply, moreover, recognizing the value of the awareness of the common faithful (*sensus fidei*) and of the signs of the times as the supreme criteria of the Church. These are to replace the interior logic of the institutions, which are too frequently directed through the use of power—the few imposing their will on the many—instead of by authority—when guidelines assert themselves through their inherent authoritativeness—and by service.

A Harmonious Implementation?

In this context it is easy to see how the reception and perhaps even the understanding of Vatican II are still in an uncertain and embryonic state. The supremacy of the word of God, the centrality of the liturgy and the Eucharist, and the commitment to communion—from the level of the parish to that of the diocese to that of the different Christian traditions—seem to have been placed at the center of the Church's life only sporadically and to an insufficient degree. Quite frequently the faithful find themselves facing bureaucracy on an overwhelming scale, among both clergy and laity. This is produced by a mistaken approach to renewal, but in reality it is the effect of a reliance upon secular institutions. There have been significant new developments for communion, such as the election of a Slavic bishop instead of the usual Italian as the successor to Peter, or the Bishop of Rome going to the people instead of waiting for the people to come to him. But there are others, such as the synod of bishops, that are clearly plagued with powerlessness. Others still, like the pastoral and presbyteral councils, appeared to have exhausted themselves after just a few years, especially in Europe.

The bishops' conferences, which played an important role in bringing Vatican II to life, now seem infested with bureaucracy and centralism, which undermine the possibility of their becoming effective signs of communion among the Churches. The tenacity with which venerable institutions like synods or catechisms have been taken up risks becoming a stale repetition without any effective impact upon ecclesial reality because of the lack of a sufficient commitment to rethink both the aims and the means of achieving them in the spirit of a courageous renewal.

Photograph reproduced by courtesy of Giuseppe Alberigo

Professor Alberigo presents a copy of one of the volumes of *History of Vatican II* to Pope John Paul II at an audience in the Vatican.

In recent decades provisions for the reform of the Roman Curia have come at a faster pace than ever before, but these have always been of marginal significance and far from introducing any effective renewal in harmony with the new conditions of the faith and ecclesial communion.

In another critical area the promising prospects for the union of the Christian Churches have become mired in a profusion of doctrinal conferences, which are inspired by a sincere desire to overcome disagreements but almost always remain an end in themselves, devoid of any creative impulse.

The profound assimilation of both the experience and the guidelines of Vatican II is a complex, long-term process. It is true that our culture is characterized by rapid consumption and a scanty memory, but there is still a need for time, measured at least in generations, to change the outlook and behavior of a large part of humanity.

The Secret Council

Finally, was there a "secret council"? Krysten Skydsgaard, a Lutheran and one of the keenest observers of the Council, has urged people to seek the "secret Council" beyond its institutional or more superficial aspects. The Council was undeniably a striving after the gospel, much more than a single episode or a pause in ecclesiastical routine. The pastoral nature of Vatican II and its efforts toward renewal lent a powerful significance to the participation of the bishops, theologians, and observers. This induces one to find in the event a profound and commonly shared experience. It is a sharing that transcended the frequently narrow and formal limitations of relationships among the ecclesiastics. Hundreds of persons who were totally unfamiliar to one another, who sometimes mistrusted one another, and who were of different ages, experience, language, and culture found themselves giving life to a common endeavor with implications far beyond the elaboration and approval of specific decisions.

From this point of view the Council was a masterpiece of the Catholic bishops and of the subtle workings of the Holy Spirit. It is, in fact, undeniable that only the profound transformation of the bishops made possible the transition (which should, perhaps, be described in terms of an overturning) from the inert and timid passivity found in the hundreds of replies sent to Rome in 1960 to the decisions approved by the Council. It is impossible not to notice the qualitative leap that took place between the survey sent back in response to the invitation from John XXIII and the image of Christianity and the Church that Vatican II expressed by virtue of the almost complete consensus among the bishops.

After 1959 there was the slow and almost imperceptible growth of a tendency among a great number of the bishops, especially those from Western Europe and North America, to understand and experience Vatican

II as a singular occasion for Church renewal, following in the path of the work done in the most recent decades by the liturgical, biblical, and ecumenical movements. The fervor of the atmosphere created in Rome by the prolonged presence of more than two thousand bishops, as many periti (theologians, canonists, historians), non-Catholic observers, and numerous journalists, played a growing role in the consciousness of the assembly. The ostentation of ecclesiastical dress and the sometimes severe cultural differences and economic disparities did not prevent the creation of a fraternal atmosphere, which may have been the hidden cause of the Council's impact upon both believers and public opinion.

This is the soil that nourished in many of the fathers an experience of their own responsibility, profoundly transforming their convictions. This is the only way to explain the constant presence of the huge majority that asserted itself in all of the crucial votes, from the sacramental nature of episcopal consecration and collegiality to Catholicism's ecumenical attitude, from the centrality of the Bible to friendship with humanity to religious liberty and relations with the Jewish people.

Could the Council have done more? From the point of view of the history of Vatican II, the question is awkward and the answer uncertain. The perspectives John XXIII raised simply by convening an ecumenical council after the one in 1870, and then specified in his opening speech, appear as demanding as they are provocative. As has been seen, the outlook of many of the Council fathers was much more limited. The hypothesis that Lercaro brought forward at the beginning of December 1962—for a Council committed to bringing evangelical poverty to life in all of its spiritual, cultural, and institutional dimensions—fell on deaf ears, in spite of the interest it had raised among the bishops of the Third World. The same fate befell the proposal advanced by Patriarch Maximos IV and seconded by many others that a permanent body representing the world's bishops collaborate with the pope on the major decisions facing the Church as a whole. The list of "omissions" could be continued . . .

And yet, Vatican II left the Catholic Church very different from the way it had found it. The condition of "Christendom," which had still been dominant in Europe and, through Europe, in worldwide Catholicism, seemed to have been jettisoned by December 8, 1965. Fragments of the old outlook still survive, and sometimes these tenaciously resist taking into account the historic transformations that occurred, but on the whole these are just little bursts of nostalgia.[2] In the long term what characterizes the shift begun by the Council is the abandonment of the Counter-Reformation and the Constantinian age. This is necessarily a complex and gradual transition, and the Council's contribution was to create a foundation for this and to signal its beginning.

The act of summoning Catholicism to a council, followed by the developments of this great assembly, aroused wide and deep interest beyond the usual ecclesial boundaries. This interest was quickly transformed into enthusiastic involvement and resulted in the creation of a "conciliar atmosphere." This atmosphere was characterized, in the first place, by eager anticipation for the decisions of the Council, and then by the willingness to change. The proof of the widespread nature of this consensus can be found in the isolation and, finally, the schism of the traditionalist followers of French Archbishop Marcel Lefebvre.

The importance of the wide reception of Vatican II, which involves not only the "official" Church—the pope, bishops, priests—but also the people of God as a whole, is shown by the general approval with which the Council's documents were met. If the impulse of the Council were to collapse back upon itself, the result will be widespread disappointment and the squandering of the extraordinarily powerful expectations and willingness accompanying this genuinely historic opportunity.

Photograph reproduced by courtesy
of Giuseppe Alberigo

Professor Giuseppe Alberigo with his wife and
coworker of many years, Angelina Nicora, at their
home in the Alps in the province of Trent during
the summer of 2001.

Notes

Preface

1. The book was published in Latin as *Conciliorum Oecumenicorum et Decreta* by Herder in Basel in 1962 and in an Italian-Latin edition in 1962 by Edizioni Dehoniane in Bologna in 1991.

2. The English edition was edited by Joseph A. Komonchak and published by Orbis Books from 1995 to 2006.

1   The Proclamation of the Council

1. The critical text was edited by Alberto Melloni, "'Questa festiva ricorrenza': Prodromi e preparazione del discorso di annuncio del Vaticano II (25 gennaio 1959)," *Rivista di Storia e Letteratura Religiosa* 28 (1992), pp. 607–43.

2. *Giornale dell' anima* notes taken July-August 1962. The English translation of the book is *Journal of a Soul*, trans. Dorothy White (New York: McGraw-Hill, 1965). The book is the spiritual diary that Roncalli kept throughout his life. A new Italian edition by Alberto Melloni was published in Bologna in 2003.

3. *Discorsi Messaggi Colloqui del S. Padre Giovanni XXIII*, 6 vols. (Vatican City: Editrice Vaticana, 1963–67), 1:250, 2:654, 4:868.

4. Eric Mahieu, ed., *Mon journal du concile* (Paris, 2002), p. 4.

5. See Loris Capovilla, "Il concilio ecumenico Vaticano II: la decisione di Giovanni XXIII: Precedenti storico et motivazioni personali," in *Come si è giunti al concilio Vaticano II*, ed. G. Galeazzi (Milan, 1988), pp. 15–60. See also Carlo Felice Casula, "Tardini e la preparazione del concilio," ibid., pp. 172–75.

6. Giuseppe De Luca to Giovanni Battista Montini, August 6, 1959, in Paolo Vian, ed., *Carteggio 1930–1962* (Brescia, 1992), p. 232.

7. Letter from Fr. Vagaggini to Giuseppe Alberigo, sent from Soci (province of Arezzo) on February 25, 1985.

8. Notes from January 26 and April 24, Fioretta Mazzei, "Giovanni XXIII transizione del papato e della chiesa," in *Giovanni XXIII and La Pira*, ed. Giuseppe Alberigo (Rome, 1988), p. 73.

9. *Acta et Documenta Concilio oecumenico Vaticano II apparando* (Typis Polyglottis Vaticanis, 1960–61), 1:16, 28.

10. Alberto Melloni, "Governi e diplomazie davanti all'annuncio del Vaticano II," in *L'altra Roma: Politica e S. Sede durante il concilio Vaticano II (1959–1965)* (Bologna, 2000), pp. 37–99.

11. See Adriano Roccucci, "Russian Observers at Vatican II: The 'Council for Russian Orthodox Church Affairs' and the Moscow Patriarchate between Antireligious Policy and International Strategies," in *Vatican II in Moscow (1959–1965)*, ed. Alberto Melloni (Leuven, 1997), pp. 45–69.

12. *Discorsi Messaggi Colloqui*, 1:903.

13. *Acta et Documenta Concilio oecumenico Vaticano II apparando*, 1:19, 24.

14. *Discorsi Messaggi Colloqui*, 4:875.

15. *Acta et Documenta Concilio oecumenico Vaticano II apparando*, 1:22–23.

16. See Antonino Indelicato, *Difendere la Dottrina o annunciare l'Evangelo: Il dibattito nella Commissione Centrale Preparatoria del Vaticano II* (Genoa, 1992).

17. See Stjepan Schmidt, "Giovanni XXIII e il Secretariato per l'unione dei cristiani," in *Christianeso* 8 (1987), pp. 95–117; and Mauro Velati, *Una difficile transizione: Il cattolicesimo tra umionismo e ecumenismo (1952–1964)* (Bologna, 1996).

18. The Latin word *schema* (plural, *schemata*) was used for the outlines or working drafts proposed to the bishops and was used in all European languages, including English.

19. Although that document, *Ordo Concilii Oecumenici Vaticani II celebrandi* (The order for celebrating the Second Vatican Ecumenical Council), is dated August 6, 1962, the document was published on September 5. Thus bishops were unable to read it until just before the beginning of their work.

2   Toward a Conciliar Consciousness

1. The text of the speech is available in English on a number of websites. The critical text, compiled on the basis of later revisions by the pope, was edited by Giuseppe Alberigo and Alberto Melloni and published as *L'allocuzione "Gaudet mater Ecclesia" di Giovanni XXIII* [John XXIII's Address *Gaudet Mater Ecclesia*], in *Fede Tradizione Profezia: Studi su Giovanni XXIII e sul Vaticano II* [Faith, Tradition, and Prophecy: Studies on John XXIII and Vatican II] (Brescia, 1984), pp. 185–283.

2. M.-D. Chenu, *Diario del Vaticano II, 1962–1963*, trans. and ed. Alberto Melloni (Bologna, 1996), October 20, 1962.

3. *Acta Synodalia Sacrosancti Concilii Vaticani II* (Vatican City: Typis Polyglottis Vaticanis, 1970–80), 1:230–32.

4. *Ordo agendorum tempore quod inter conclusionem primae periodi concilii oecumenici et initium secundae intercedit* (The Order for Proceeding in the Interval between the First Session of the Council and the Beginning of the Second), in *Acta Synodalia*, 1:96–98.

5. The documentation produced by this definitive group is collected in volume five of *Acta Synodalia*.

6. All these texts are collected in Giuseppe Alberigo and Franca Magistretti, eds., *Constitutionis dogmaticae "Lumen Gentium" Synopsis Historica* (Historical Synopsis of the Dogmatic Constitution "Lumen Gentium") (Bologna, 1975).

7. *Translator's note*—We follow the practice of referring to Council documents by the first letters of their Latin titles, using the article numbers of the official text to refer to particular passages. English quotations are from Austin Flannery, ed., *Vatican Council II*, 2 vols. (Northport, NY: Costello Publishing Company, 1996).

8. See Valeria Martano, ed., *Athenagoras, il patriarca (1882–1972): Un cristiano tra crisi della coabitazione e utopia ecumenica* (Bologna, 1996).

3   The Council Matures

1. Diary of Angelina Nicora, October 21, 1963.
2. Letter sent from Bologna by Angelina Nicora to Dossetti, October 15, 1963.
3. Diary of Angelina Nicora, October 21, 1963.
4. Ibid.
5. Ibid., November 19, 1963.
6. Ibid., December 28, 1963.
7. See Giuseppe Dossetti, *Per una "Chiesa eucaristica": Rilettura della portata dottrinale della costituzione liturgica del Vaticano II* (Toward a "Eucharistic Church": A Rereading of the Doctrinal Impact of the Liturgical Constitution of Vatican II), ed. Giuseppe Alberigo and Giuseppe Ruggieri (Bologna, 2001).
8. Diary of Angelina Nicora, October 21, 1963.

4   The Church Is a Communion

1. Diary of Angelina Nicora, December 1, 1963.
2. The Italian title was *Lo sviluppo della dottrina sui poteri nella chiesa universale: Momenti essenziali tra il XVI e il XIX secolo* (The Development of the Doctrine on Powers in the Universal Church: Essential Moments between the Sixteenth and Nineteenth Centuries).
3. Diary of Angelina Nicora, January 26, 1965.
4. Ibid., October 21, 1963.
5. Dossetti Archive, II:100; it was also included in *Cristianesimo nella storia* 8 (1987), pp. 161–62.
6. Diary of Bishop Vicente Zaspe, November 19, 1964.
7. Luis A. G. Tagle, "The 'Black Week' of Vatican II," in *History of Vatican II*, 5 vols., ed. Giuseppe Alberigo and Joseph A. Komonchak (Maryknoll, NY: Orbis Books, 1995–2006), 4:452.
8. See Giovanni Turbanti, *Un concilio per il mondo moderno: La redazione della costituzione pastorale* "Gaudium et spes" *del Vaticano II* (A Council for the Modern World: The Drafting of the Vatican Council II Pastoral Constitution *Gaudium et Spes*) (Bologna, 2000).
9. This is what Alexandra von Teuffenbach does in *Die Bedeutung des "subsistit in" (LG 8): Zum Selbstverständnis der katholischen Kirche* (Munich, 2002). For an appropriate critique of her interpretation, see Luigi Sartori, "Osservazioni sull'ermeneutica del 'subsistit in' proposta da Alexandra von Teuffenbach," *Rassegna de Teologia* 45 (2004), pp. 279–81.

5   The Faith Lives within History

1. Diary of Angelina Nicora, February 21–28, 1965.
2. The text is found in *Discorsi conciliari del card: Giacomo Lercaro: Per la forza dello Spirito* (Conciliar Speeches of Cardinal Giacomo Lercaro: By the Power of the Spirit) (Bologna, 1984), pp. 287–310. The lecture was articulated in six points: (1) the supernatural unity of his [John XXIII's] being and action; (2) an assessment

of his overall tendencies; (3) his "cultural" preparation; (4) the decision to be a teacher and guide; (5) John and the Council; and (6) the holiness of John XXIII.

3. Franz König, *La Civiltà Cattolica* 116/2 (1965), pp. 490–92.

4. Letter from Raniero La Valle to Giuseppe Alberigo, sent from Bologna on July 25, 1965.

5. See Massimo Faggioli, *Il vescovo e il concilio: Modello episcopale e aggiornamento nella storia del decreto "Christus Dominus"* (The Bishop and the Council: The Episcopal Model and Renewal in the History of the Vatican II Decree *Christus Dominus*) (Bologna, 2005).

6. See Riccardo Burigana, *La bibbia nel concilio: La redazione della costituzione Dei Verbum"*(The Bible at the Council: The Drafting of the Constitution *Dei Verbum* of Vatican II) (Bologna, 1998).

7. Cf. Silvia Scatena, *La fatica della libertà: L'elaborazione della dichiarazione "Dignitatis humanae"* (Freedom Is Hard Work: The Elaboration of Vatican II's Constitution on Religious Liberty *Dei Verbum*) (Bologna, 2002).

8. Paul VI created the international synod in *Apostolica Sollicitudo*, his Motu Proprio of September 15, 1965.

6 *For the Renewal of Christianity*

1. See *Concilium* 13 (1977), pp. 163–66.

2. See Gianfranco Bottoni, ed., *Fine della Christianità? Christianesimo tra religione civile e tetsimonianza evangelica* (The End of Christendom? Christianity between Civil Religion and Evangelical Witness) (Bologna, 2002).

Important Dates Connected
with Vatican II

1959   January 25—John XXIII announces his decision to call a new council

1959   Beginning of the pre-preparatory phase

1959   July 14—Decision to call the council "Vatican II"

1960   January 24–31—The Roman synod

1960   June 5—Appointment of the preparatory commissions

1960   July—Drafting of the "Questions Posed to the Preparatory Commissions"

1961   June—Beginning of the work of the Central Preparatory Commission

1962   February 2—John XXIII sets November 11, 1962, as the start date for the Council

1962   September 11—John XXIII's radio message "Lumen Christi—Ecclesia Christi"

1962   October 11—Opening of the Council in St. Peter's; opening address by John XXIII, *Gaudet Mater Ecclesia*

1962   October 20—The Council's message to humanity

1962   November 20—A majority of the Council rejects the project on the two sources of revelation

1962   December 12—The concluding session for the first period

1962–63   The second preparation for the Council

1963   January 6—John XXIII's letter to the bishops, *Mirabilis Ille*

1963   April 11—Encyclical *Pacem in Terris*

1963   June 3—Death of John XXIII

1963   June 21—Election of Paul VI

1963   September 29—Opening of the Council's second period

1963   October 30—Preliminary voting on *De Ecclesia*

1963   December 4—The concluding session of the second period; approval of the *Constitution on the Sacred Liturgy (Sacrosanctum Concilium)* and the *Decree on the Means of Social Communication (Inter Mirifica)*

1964   January 4–6—Pilgrimage of Paul VI to Jerusalem and his meeting with Patriarch Athenagoras

1964   January 25—Creation of the "Council for the implementation of the liturgical constitution"

1964   Opening of the third period of the Council

1964   November 14–21—Black Week

1964   November 21—Concluding session of the third period; approval of the *Dogmatic Constitution on the Church (Lumen Gentium)*, the *Decrees on Ecumenism (Unitatis Reintegration)*, and the *Decree on the Eastern Catholic Churches (Orientalium Ecclesiarum)*

1965   March 7—Inauguration of the reformed Eucharistic liturgy

1965   September 14—Opening of the fourth period of the Council

1965   October 28—Approval of the *Decree on the Bishops' Pastoral Office in the Church (Christus Dominus)*, the *Decree on the Appropriate Renewal of Religious Life (Perfectae Caritatis)*, the *Decree on Priestly Formation (Optatam Totius)*, the *Declaration on Christian Education (Gravissimum Educationis)*, and the *Declaration on Religious Freedom (Nostra Aetate)*

1965   November 18—Approval of the *Dogmatic Constitution on Divine Revelation (Dei Verbum)* and the *Decree on the Apostolate of the Laity (Apostolicam Actuositatem)*

1965   December 7—Concluding session of the fourth and final period;
                    approval of the *Pastoral Constitution on the Church in the Modern
                    World (Gaudium et Spes)*, the *Decree on the Missionary Activity of the
                    Church (Ad Gentes)*, the *Decree on the Ministry and Life of Priests
                    (Presbyterorum Ordinis)*, and the *Declaration on the Relationship of
                    the Church to the Non-Christian Religions (Dignitatis Humanae)*

1965   December 8—Final celebration with the reading of the messages
                    for humanity

Index of Names

A

Agagianian, P. G., 32, 36
Alberigo, G., vii, viii, 22, 67, 72, 121, 127, 130
Alfrink, B., x, 101, 106
Aquinas, Thomas, 123
Athenagoras, Patriarch, 7, 40, 57, 60, 66, 136

B

Bacci, A., 28
Bea, A., x, 13, 16, 27, 41, 57, 70, 72, 93, 199, 121
Beran, J., 99, 100
Bertrams, W., 58
Bettazzi, L., 44, 101
Bismarck, O., von, 46
Brand, P., 40
Bugnini, A., 5, 61
Butler, B. C., 51

C

Câmara, H., 41, 118
Cantimori, D., x
Carli, L. M., 52, 68
Chenu, M.-D., 20, 24, 100
Cicognani, A., 32, 48, 58, 90, 98, 121
Colombo, C., 52, 58, 69, 74, 75
Confalonieri, C. 32
Congar, I., x, 2, 10, 20, 41, 71, 102
Cushing, R. J., 69

D

Danielou, J., 41
de Lubac, H. 20, 70
D'Souza, E. 51
De Luca, G., 5

De Smedt, E., 30, 69, 99
Döpfner, J., 30, 32, 36, 58, 82, 106
Dossetti, G., vii, ix, x, xi, 24, 26, 44, 46, 47, 48, 49, 52, 53, 65, 67, 72, 74, 93
Duprey, P., x, 66
Duval, L. É., 101

E

Einaudi, L., 46

F

Felici, P., 5, 11, 41, 48, 73, 90
Frings, J., 24, 41, 51, 73, 74

G

Gagnebet, R., 47
Garrone, G., 100
Gauthier, P., 26
Gracias, V., 37
Greco, G., 41, 89, 103
Guano, E., 79
Guitton, J., 72

H

Hus, J., 100

I

Iakovos, K., 7
Illich, I., 49

J

Jedin, H., ix, x, 36
Jerome, St., 108
John Paul II, 127